JOHN

Look through Luke

Published in Great Britain by
Henry E. Walter Ltd.
26 Grafton Road, Worthing, England. BN11 1QU

Published in United States by
Lamb Publications, Inc.
30 Broadway Square, Mesquite, Texas U.S.A. 75150

©John Blanchard 1977
first published 1977
U.K. ISBN 0-85479-701-7
U.S.A. ISBN 0-89597-001-5
Library of Congress No. 77-84306

Printed in the U.S.A. by...
Lamb Publications, Inc.

Introduction

. Some years ago I wrote a book called READ MARK LEARN, a series of Bible reading notes for people beginning the Christian life. It covered the Gospel of Mark in 45 daily readings, and was written because I was convinced that in spite of the existence of a number of Bible reading "systems" there was a specific need for a book deliberately written with the new Christian in mind.

To my great surprise, I discovered that the book was not only being used to help those beginning the Christian life, but by many who had been Christians for years. In addition, it was being used in group activities such as house meetings, youth camps, church Bible studies and the like — to say nothing of its use by hard-pressed preachers in search of sermon outlines!

As a result, not only has READ MARK LEARN now run to eleven editions in as many years, but there has been an increasing demand for another book to succeed it, and specifically for a book on another of the Gospels. This outside pressure has coincided with a deepening conviction of my own that many Christians have no regular guidelines for their personal Bible reading, or are dissatisfied with the system they are using. LOOK THROUGH LUKE is the outcome of these combined pressures.

The format of the book will already be obvious, but there are a few points that I would like to make by way of specific introduction.

Firstly, the notes are about twice the length of those in READ MARK LEARN, and this is quite deliberate. My guess is that as far as personal daily Bible reading is concerned a disturbing number of Christians are making do with what we could call "a look and a promise." My earnest hope is that LOOK THROUGH LUKE will help many of them to move away from this hit and miss business to a much more sustained approach. As a very rough guideline, my hope would be that a Christian using these notes would be prepared to take 20-30 minutes in carefully following through the reading and notes set out for each day.

Secondly, I have deliberately refrained from using quotations or illustrations from any other source except the Bible itself. There would have been nothing wrong in doing so, of course, but in preparing these studies my great concern has been to *let the Bible speak for itself*. It is always exhilarating to see how wonderfully God's Word fits together, and I hope that those using these notes will share in that experience.

Thirdly, a word about translations. We live at a time when we are deluged with translations and paraphrases of the Bible, and any preacher or writer has to try to come to terms with the situation. In preparing these notes, my policy has been as follows: I have based the readings on the *Authorised Version,* which I still find to be the most widely used of all the translations currently available. Then, whenever it has been necessary to use another version either to bring out the meaning of a phrase more accurately, or to avoid the archaic language of the Authorised Version, I have basically used two others. The first is the *New International Version (NIV),* which may yet prove to be the best of all the recent translations. However, only the New Testament is available in the NIV at the moment, so for the Old Testament I have where necessary used the *Revised Standard Version (RSV).* Very occasionally, when I have felt that its particular choice of words has been helpful in bringing out the full meaning of a phrase, I have used *The Amplified Bible (AMP).* The battle of the versions will no doubt be with us for a long time yet, but I hope that my choice and use of these will produce the maximum of help with the minimum of confusion.

As with **READ MARK LEARN,** these notes may

prove helpful in group activities, but they have been written with the individual reader primarily in mind. That being so, let me repeat the very basic suggestions I made in the Introduction to READ MARK LEARN as to how they should be used:—

1. As you come to the Bible each day, take time to pray that God will help you to understand what you are about to read.

2. Read slowly and carefully the passage indicated in the top right hand corner of the page.

3. Read the notes for that day, looking back to the passage in Luke whenever a particular verse or phrase is quoted, and looking up every other Bible reference as it is mentioned.

4. Look up the text quoted at the foot of the page and think about how it fits in with the day's reading.

5. Keep a notebook handy, and jot down anything you think is especially helpful or relevant to your own life.

6. Pray that God will help you to live out the implications of whatever particular truths he has impressed upon you during your time of study and meditation.

The Gospel of Luke is a very exciting book, not least because it points its readers clearly and constantly to the Lord Jesus Christ as man's all-sufficient Saviour. My prayer is that these notes will help many people to follow Luke's directions.

CROYDON,
England.   JOHN BLANCHARD
September 1977

1
God Speaking
Luke 1.1-17

When reading and studying the Bible, nothing is more important than to realise that it is *God's Word,* and not merely a collection of religious ideas put together by good men. The authority of the Bible comes not from the calibre of its human authors, but from the character of its Divine author, the living and eternal God. This all-important truth about the authority of Scripture comes across in two ways in today's opening reading in Luke's Gospel.

The Word That Comes From God It is always interesting to notice the immediate purpose for which certain parts of the Bible were written (two clear examples of this are John 20.30-31 and 1 John 5.13). In the passage before us we discover that Luke wrote his book to a man called Theophilus, who may have been an important official, judging by the way Luke addressed him (v.3); and the purpose of his writing was to confirm in the mind of Theophilus the things he had already been told (v.4). But how did Luke know these things? First of all, he knew them by *revelation;* he speaks of "the things that have been fulfilled among us" (v.1 NIV). Christianity is not based on ideas, but on events, and in those events God fulfilled promises he had already given. Then Luke knew these things by *confirmation;* he says "the facts were handed down to us by those who from the very first were eyewitnesses (and "ear-witnesses"!) of what he had said and done (compare 1 John 1.1-3 and 2 Peter 1.16-18). Finally, Luke knew these things by *investigation;* he says "I myself have carefully investigated everything from the beginning" (v.3 NIV). Now Luke was a doctor (see Colossians 4.14), a man used to making close examinations, and unlikely to lend his name to vague theories and superstitions. As you study his book you will discover that Luke is a stickler for *facts* and *details*. That is precisely why he set out to write "an orderly account" (v.3 NIV) of the events that had shaken the world.

The Word That Came Through Gabriel Luke begins his account with an unlikely couple, an elderly priest called Zechariah and his wife Elizabeth. They were godly in life (v.6) but to their great sorrow they were childless (v.7). When Zechariah was on duty in the temple one day, an angel suddenly appeared to him (vv.8-11). Needless to say, the old man was "gripped with fear" (v.12 NIV), but the angel told him the great news that Elizabeth was to have a son (v.13). Notice that this was specifically said to be in answer to prayer. Notice, too, that Zechariah was given one clear instruction — the child was to be called John. Then came a series of amazing prophecies about this unborn child. He would be a cause of great delight to many people (v.14), he would be counted great even in God's eyes (v.15), he would exercise great personal discipline (v.15) and be filled with the Holy Spirit from his birth (v.15). His life's work would be similar to that of the great prophet Elijah, calling people to repentance; and as a result many disobedient Jews would turn back to God (vv. 16-17). This prophecy was fulfilled to the letter (see Matthew 3.1-3) — because as we shall see more fully in our next study, the word that came through Gabriel was a word that came from God. God still speaks today, through creation, world events, the lives of Christians, and in many other ways; but he speaks most clearly through his infallible, unchanging word, the Bible (see Psalm 19.7-9).

"All scripture is given by inspiration of God" (2 Timothy 3.16).

2
Man Responding
Luke 1.18-25

The angel's prophecy had been astonishing—surely too good to be true? With simple honesty, Luke now records the reaction of Zechariah and Elizabeth. Three words will help us to sum these up.

Doubtful Zechariah surely *wanted* to believe his ears, but he had one major difficulty — surely both he and Elizabeth were too old to have a child? (v.18). His response was natural—but he had missed the point that the message was supernatural. The angel answered "I am Gabriel. I stand in the presence of God" (v.19 NIV). The angel's message came from heaven, not from hospital! Zechariah's unbelief was made more serious by the fact that he was refusing to accept that God had answered prayer. There is another illustration of this at Acts 12 — see especially vv.5 and 12-16. The God we worship is the God of the impossible, who is "able to do immeasurably more than all we ask or imagine, according to his power that is at work within us" (Ephesians 3.20 NIV). We dare not limit him in our asking, nor in his answering.

Dumb Gabriel's (and therefore God's) response to Zechariah's unbelief was sudden and severe. He was to be struck dumb as a direct result of his unbelief, and would not regain his voice until the promised child had been born (v.20). What a vivid lesson about the importance of taking God at his word! There are other New Testament illustrations of this: Matthew 13.58 and Mark 6.5-6, for instance. God has inserted the principle of *faith* into his dealings with men, and none of the blessings of the gospel are possible without it: "Without faith it is impossible to please God, because anyone who comes to him must believe that he exists and that he rewards those who earnestly seek him" (Hebrews 11.6 NIV). If only we knew how much blessing we missed, or how much loss we suffered, because of our downright unbelief, we would surely be ashamed!

Delighted The spotlight now switches to Elizabeth who, some time later, discovered that she was expecting a baby (v.24). It is interesting how Elizabeth's reaction differed from that of her husband. Her immediate response was "The Lord has done this for me" (v.25 NIV). There is no suggestion here that this was to be a virgin birth; it is clear that Zechariah was the father of the child. The remarkable thing about it was that God had graciously given Elizabeth special enabling to conceive, carry and give birth to the child at an advanced age. But Elizabeth went on to say that the Lord had done something else — "he has shown his favour and taken away my disgrace among the people" (v.25 NIV). To the Jews, childlessness was not merely sad, it was significant. It was a sign of God's disfavour. A man could even divorce his wife if she did not bear him children. Because of this Elizabeth had spent years in disgrace, with people mocking her barrenness, and inferring that this was a judgment on her sin. There is another example of this heartless thinking at John 9.1-2. It is certainly true that all affliction can be traced back to the original sin of Adam; it is true that the sins of the parents are sometimes visited on their children; it is also true that one's own sins can be a direct cause of suffering; but it is *not* true that every affliction is the direct result of a particular sin. Pain and suffering are not necessarily signs of God's anger; Proverbs 3.11-12 and Revelation 3.19 tell us that the exact opposite is sometimes the case. For Elizabeth, only one thing mattered; she had found favour with God. No Christian could have a greater concern than that! (see 1 Thessalonians 4.1).

"A good man obtains favour from the Lord" (Proverbs 12.2 RSV).

3
God's Mysterious Ways
Luke 1.26-38

In today's reading, Luke continues to establish the background to everything else that he is to write. So far, the action has taken place in Jerusalem and an un-named town in Judea. Now we move on six months, and the scene switches to a town called Nazareth in Galilee. Here we find a young woman called Mary, a relative of Elizabeth (v.36) who was "pledged to be married to a man named Joseph" (v.27 NIV). The action can now be captured in four paragraphs.

A Message Is Announced Again, the angel Gabriel was the messenger (v.26) and his message to Mary was truly amazing. Firstly, he told her that in a very special way she had "found favour with God" (v.30). On hearing this, Mary was speechless, unable to grasp what this meant (v.29). Notice carefully that she was startled not so much by the angel's appearance, but by his *words*. She was stunned to think that she had found favour with God — a lovely lesson in humility. But the heart of the angel's message was even more startling; like Elizabeth, she was to give birth to a son, in this case to be called Jesus (v.31). We shall return to the rest of the angel's message later.

A Miracle Is Assumed Mary's first words to the angel were "How can this be, since I am a virgin?" (v.34 NIV) Whereas Zechariah did not believe the angel, Mary *did* believe him, but was naturally puzzled as to how such a thing could be achieved. It is a sin to doubt that God will do what he says, but not to admit ignorance of how he will do it. The angel's answer to Mary's question was breathtaking (v.35). There was to be a biological mira-cle, resulting in what we now call the virgin birth. The *power* by which God did this was the power of the Holy

Spirit; the *principle* under which he did it is that "nothing is impossible with God" (v.37 NIV).

The Messiah Is Anticipated The Old Testament is full of prophecies about God sending the Messiah (which means The Anointed One). Amazingly, the first veiled prophecy was made to the devil! (see Genesis 3.15). Notice that the one who would eventually conquer the devil would be the seed of the *woman* (whereas one normally speaks of the seed of a man). From then on, one detail after another was added until we come towards the last of the prophecies before the Messiah came (vv.32-33 and 35). Notice particularly that the child was to be "holy" in his character, something impossible if he was conceived in the normal way (see Psalm 51.5 and Ephesians 2.3). He was to be without human failure because he was to be without a human father. In a way true of no other person, he would be called "the Son of God" (v.35).

The Mystery Is Accepted However marvellous all this sounded to Mary, it remained staggeringly mysterious. Yet at the end of the day, she accepted it all. Her final words to the angel were "I am the Lord's servant. May it be to me as you have said" (v.38 NIV). There were many things she could not understand, but nothing that she was not prepared to accept. There is an important lesson here for all Christians. We are not always clear as to what God is doing with our lives. God's ways are mysterious and sometimes perplexing or painful. Yet we are called upon always to submit to his "good and acceptable and perfect will" (Romans 12.2) whatever that might mean. Even the question of whether we live or die then becomes immaterial! (see Philippians 1.20).

"As for God, his way is perfect" (Psalm 18.30)

4
Magnificat!
Luke 1.39-56

Our last study ended with Mary humbly submitting to the angel Gabriel's astonishing message. Yet the whole experience must have been a very testing one, and Mary decided to take a three months' break at Elizabeth's home in the hill country of Judea (vv.39-40 and 56). Today's reading covers all we know of their time together.

The Welcome Elizabeth Gave The setting is a very homely one with two mothers-to-be sharing those things nearest to their hearts. Yet there is profound spiritual truth locked up in it all. The first thing that stands out in Elizabeth's welcome is that she showed no jealousy whatever. She immediately acknowledged Mary as being "Blessed — favoured of God — above all other women" (v.42 AMP). Elizabeth was older, and had herself been greatly honoured by God; but she did not make any capital out of these. In fact, she counted herself unworthy even to receive Mary as a guest (v.43). Notice how closely this compares with what John himself said about Jesus many years later (see Matthew 3.14). Finally, Elizabeth's welcome showed that she had great faith. She was not only absolutely certain that God would perform all that he had promised (v.45) but she also believed that Mary's unborn child was her own "Lord" (v.43). The reason for Elizabeth's spirituality and insight is not hard to find — she was "filled with the Holy Spirit" (v.41).

The Worship Mary Offered The section containing verses 46-55 is sometimes called the Magnificat (from the Latin of the opening words) and is still sung in churches all over the world today. In it, we can trace at least three of the attributes of God. Firstly there is his majesty (vv.46, 47 and 49). Make a special note of the fact that Mary acknowledged God as her Savior (v.47) which meant that she knew herself to be a sinner. What shines out from this passage is not the sinlessness of Mary, but the sovereign majesty of God, of whom alone it can be said "holy is his name". Secondly, we see the tremendous power of God (v.49). Mary began on a personal level, and said that God had done "great things" for her (v.49); but then she moved on to the much wider truth that God had "performed mighty deeds with his arm" (v.51 NIV). Nobody has a correct view of the world or of history until they can see that God is at work. Mary then developed this overall truth in two ways. *God exalts and humbles* (vv.51-52); all kings and kingdoms are under God's sovereign control, and even the worst of despots is subject to his power (link Psalm 22.28 and Proverbs 8.15 with Exodus 9.16). *God enriches and impoverishes* (v.53); if it pleases God's purposes he can bring a millionaire to the breadline, and set up a pauper in a palace. Our health and wealth are in God's hands—which is why Paul was able to say what he did at Philippians 4.11-12. Thirdly, we see the wonderful mercy of God (vv.50 and 54-55). Notice that God's mercy is said to be based on his word—it is "even as he said to our fathers" (v.55 NIV). The Old Testament promises must have seemed just ancient history to many of the Jews, but God had not forgotten, and was acting "in remembrance of his mercy" (v.54). Mary saw what was about to happen as the fulfilment of God's pledge to bless his people. God's promises of mercy are just as real today. Isaiah 55.6-7 and 2 Chronicles 7.14 are among the most marvellous words any person could ever read, and the greatest promises any person could ever claim.

"O magnify the Lord with me, and let us exalt his name together" (Psalm 34.3).

5
Benedictus!
Luke 1.57-80

In today's reading, Luke completes setting the scene for
the coming of the Messiah by describing the events
surrounding the birth of John, which took place a little
earlier. The passage divides very naturally into an introduction and a benediction.

Introduction Luke begins by telling us that in due
course "Elizabeth's full time came" (v.57). Primarily, of
course, he meant that she gave birth about nine months
after conception; but the fuller meaning is that John
arrived exactly according to God's schedule. Elizabeth
was proving to the hilt the kind of promise made at
Joshua 23.14. When the happy event took place, her
neighbours and relatives "shared her joy" (v.58); a welcome change of spirit from verse 24! According to Old
Testament law, male children were circumcised on the
eighth day (Genesis 17.12). This was also the day when
the child would be named. People assumed that he
would be called Zechariah, after his father (that seems
to be the meaning of the end of v.59); but Elizabeth
interrupted them to say that he was to be called John
(v.60). They were obviously puzzled about this, and
turned to Zechariah for his choice (vv.61-62). To their
amazement, he immediately wrote "His name is John"
(v.63). By now he had obviously realised that God was in
this whole matter, and that his responsibility was unqualified obedience to the clear instructions he had
been given (see v.13). Immediately, the result of his
disobedience was removed (v.64); God did not press his
judgment against him a moment longer than was necessary. In turn, Zechariah's first words were of praise and
worship (vv.67-68, and compare Noah's actions at
Genesis 8.18-20 immediately after the flood had sub-
sided).

Benediction Zechariah's words are sometimes called the Benedictus (the Latin of the opening phrase). The first thing for which Zechariah gave thanks was that God had "visited and redeemed his people". Although he must at that moment have been the proudest father in Israel, the subject of his praise was not John but Jesus! His great theme was that God had at last fulfilled his promise, and that the Messiah had come (though Jesus was still in his mother's womb at the time). He then used several vivid phrases to describe the coming child and to show that amazing things he was to accomplish. For instance, he would be "a horn of salvation" (v.69) — a horn being a symbol of strength; and as such he would save his people from their enemies (v.71). No human mind can grasp the tremendous power needed to deliver even one person from the guilt and grip of sin, yet Jesus was to do this for countless multitudes. Then he was described as "the Highest" and "the Lord" (v.76), titles which could only speak of deity; and it was because of this that he was able to fulfil God's covenant promises (vv.72-73). Thirdly, he was given the title "the dayspring from on high" (v.78); and as such he would "shine on those living in darkness and in the shadow of death" (v.79 NIV). Compare this with what Jesus himself said later (John 8.12) and with what Paul added at 2 Corinthians 4.3-4. As the sun gives light to the earth, so Jesus gives light to the soul. Yet a personal response was called for. The purpose of our deliverance by Christ was that we might "serve him without fear in holiness and righteousness before him all our days" (vv.74-75 NIV). God's claims on the redeemed sinner are not only moral and spiritual, but *total*.

"For you were once darkness, but now you are light in the Lord. Live as children of light" (Ephesians 5.8 NIV).

6
God Breaks Through
Luke 2.1-20

Having carefully sketched in the background as part of the "orderly account" he was writing to Theophilus, Luke now sets out to describe the stupendous event which turned the tide of history, the moment when God broke into the world in a unique and astonishing way. We can draw the threads of Luke's record together in three paragraphs.

The Edict From Rome Luke begins by timing things in the context of other events. In this case, he notes the fact that the Roman Emperor, Caesar Augustus, had "issued a decree that a census should be taken of the entire Roman world" (v.1 NIV) and adds that one particular census took place "while Quirinius was governor of Syria" (v.2 NIV). These censuses were taken every fourteen years, with the results being used mainly for taxation purposes. Yet the Emperor's edict, together with all the local administrative arrangements, were now to fit perfectly into God's plan. People were required to register in their own home town (v.3), which for Joseph meant a long journey from Nazareth to Bethlehem, the capital city of Judea (v.4). By this time, he had married Mary (see Matthew 1.24-25), and her baby was due very soon (v.5). Normally, she might have been excused this long journey, but there was nothing normal about this particular situation! Hundreds of years before, God had decreed that the Messiah would be born in Bethlehem (see Micah 5.2); the last of the pieces was now falling perfectly into place! The actual birth of Jesus is recorded in a handful of words. With the town full of visitors taking part in the Roman census, even an expectant mother had to take whatever accommodation she could find (vv.6-7).

The Message From Heaven Meantime, other people were going about their normal business, and these included shepherds guarding their flocks in the nearby fields (v.8). Suddenly, they were dazzled and terrified by the appearance of an angel (v.9). But the angel brought "good news of great joy" ((v.10). That very day, a child had been born in Bethlehem who was "Saviour", "Christ" and "Lord" (v.11). The word "Christ" is the Greek word for "Messiah" and the word "Lord" was used as God's own name; to bring both names together put the new-born child's identity beyond all doubt! God himself had broken into history in a way that would affect "all people" (v.10). This mighty Saviour was to transform the lives of multitudes; and the day will come when his praises will be sung by those "redeemed ... to God ... out of every kindred, and tongue, and people, and nation" (Revelation 5.9). No wonder a great army of angels suddenly surrounded the shepherds praising God and promising that there would be peace on earth "to men on whom his favour rests" (v.14 NIV).

The News From Bethlehem The shepherds were not given instructions to visit Jesus, but the angels obviously assumed they would (v.12) and they did (vv.15-16). Shepherds were amongst the lowest paid of the working classes, and in some ways were social outcasts. Yet they were chosen by God to be among the very first people to see the infant Jesus. What is more, they were also among the first evangelists of his birth (v.17). Even when they returned to their normal place of work, they could not keep their experience to themselves, but shared it in a spirit of praise and worship (v.20). They were not professional preachers or gifted scholars; but they could share what they knew! Acts 4.20 and 1 John 1.3 point to every Christian having the same privilege and responsibility.

"For the grace of God that brings salvation has appeared to all men"
(Titus 2.11 NIV)

7
Nunc Dimittis!
Luke 2.21-40

Luke had already described the day when John was circumcised and named (1.59-60). As part of his "orderly account", he now records the same moment in the life of Jesus, a day marked, as was John's, by extraordinary statements of divine truth. Basically, two very significant things happened.

The Law Was Fulfilled As we have already seen, circumcision was in accordance with Jewish law (Genesis 17.12). As with John, the choice of the child's name did not rest with the parents; there had been specific instructions from God (see Matthew 1.21). The name "Jesus" was in common use (see Colossians 4.11), but in this case the naming of the child was both miraculous and full of meaning. The word "Jesus" means "God is salvation", and was therefore the perfect human name for man's divine Saviour. Another Jewish law taught that every firstborn son was consecrated to God (link v.23 with Exodus 13.2, 12 and 15). This was a reminder of God's goodness in sparing the Jews when he destroyed the firstborn of the Egyptians (see Exodus 12.29). The law went on to say that the child must then be symbolically "redeemed" by the payment of five shekels (see Num. 18.15-16) — and in order to do this Joseph and Mary took Jesus to Jerusalem (v.22). Yet another law concerned the purification of the mother. After the birth of a male child, the mother was ceremonially unclean for forty days (see Leviticus 12.1-4), after which she must offer "a lamb a year old for a burnt offering, and a young pigeon or a turtledove for a sin offering" (Leviticus 12.6 RSV). If she could not afford a lamb, a second pigeon or turtledove would be sufficient. The priest would then sacrifice the animals and pronounce the woman clean (see Leviticus 12.8). In the light of this, verse 24 tells us something about Joseph and Mary's financial position. In all of these details, Jesus was identified with those he himself had come to redeem (link verse 38 with Galatians 4.4).

The Lord Was Revealed Also in Jerusalem was a godly man called Simeon, who longed for the coming of the Messiah, and had been given a remarkable promise that he would see him before he died (vv.25-26). Led by the Holy Spirit, he was in the Temple when Joseph and Mary entered (v.27). As soon as he saw Jesus, he took him in his arms and praised God in words sometimes called the Nunc Dimittis (the opening words in Latin). As with the hymns of Mary and Zechariah, the great theme of Simeon's song was "salvation" (v.30) which was to be announced to "all people" and would be a blessing both to Jews and Gentiles (v.32). Simeon was so sure that Jesus was the Messiah that he would gladly have died there and then! (v.29) Joseph and Mary were amazed that this stranger should know such things (v.33) Then Simeon made these prophecies about Jesus: he would mean damnation to some and salvation to others; he would meet great opposition; men's reactions to him would reveal their true spiritual condition; and something (obviously his death) would cause great sorrow to Mary (check all of this with vv.34-35). Immediately after this, a devout old prophetess called Anna came up to them and gave thanks to God. After this one brief encounter, she constantly spoke about Jesus to all those who were eagerly waiting for the Messiah to come (vv.36-38). For her, as for Simeon, the wait was over!

"The Spirit of truth ... will guide you into all truth" (John 16.13).

8
Spiritual Wisdom
Luke 2.41-52

One of the most unusual things about the biography of Jesus is that from an ordinary human viewpoint it seems so uneven. There are about three chapters dealing with the events surrounding his birth, and then almost nothing for about 30 years. The only incident recorded about Jesus between his babyhood and his manhood is the one contained in today's reading when Jesus was twelve years old (v.42). In the course of our previous study we noticed that Mary and Joseph were devout and disciplined in their religion (glance back to v.39 again). As such, they would piously seek to keep all the established requirements regarding attendance at the great Jewish festivals. The law required all males to attend three times a year — at the feast of Unleavened Bread (or the Passover), at Pentecost, and at the Feast of Tabernacles (see Exodus 23.14-17). This is the background to what we read in vv.41-42. The family was in Jerusalem in compliance with the law of God; on this occasion to celebrate the Passover which commemorated the Israelites deliverance from the Egyptians (see Exodus 12.1-14).

Misunderstanding The festival lasted a week (see Exodus 13.6) and when it was over the party from Nazareth started for home (v.43). We are not told how many people travelled together on the excursion from Nazareth, but the group was obviously large enough for Mary and Joseph to travel all day without being particularly concerned that they had not seen Jesus since they left the city. It was only at the end of the day that they realised their mistake (v.44). A Christian can make the same kind of careless mistake with regard to his spiritual condition. Revelation 3.17 can be deeply challenging on this point! Never be satisfied with "supposing" that the

Lord is with you in life's decisions and directions. The right attitude for a safe and happy journey is found in 2 Peter 1.1-10!

Understanding Having failed to find Jesus among their relatives and friends (v.45), the distraught parents made their way back to Jerusalem. When they eventually found him, he was in the Temple, engaged in deep discussion with the leading religious teachers of the day. Although Jesus was not even a teenager, the scholars were "astonished and overwhelmed with bewildered wonder at his intelligence and his replies" (v.47 AMP). By his searching questions and superb answers Jesus showed himself to have an understanding of spiritual matters far beyond his years. Colossians 2.3 explains why!

No Understanding In spite of all they had seen and heard at the time of his birth, Joseph and Mary were baffled by all of this; they were "astonished" (v.48 NIV). Mary blamed Jesus for getting lost, rather than accepting the blame for losing him (v.48), and they obviously did not understand what he meant by saying "I must be about my Father's business" (v.49). As we saw in our previous study, a developing knowledge of God's will and ways is essential if life is to make any real sense. Without this spiritual understanding life becomes clouded and confusing. Incidentally, make careful note that in this passage we have Jesus's first recorded words (in v.49) — and they speak of perfect obedience to his Father's will. Psalm 40.8 should be the corresponding characteristic of the Christian.

"Wisdom is better than strength" *(Ecclesiastes 9.16).*

9
The P.R. Man
Luke 3.1-20

Having given us one fascinating glimpse of Jesus as he
approached his teenage years, and told us in a phrase or
two about his disciplined and spiritual family life at
Nazareth (look back to the last two verses of the previous chapter), Luke now takes up the story of "John, son
of Zechariah" (v.2 NIV). The last mention of John had
been about 18 years earlier; all we know of him in the
meantime is what we read at 1.80. Now it was time for
John's public ministry to begin, and Luke, with his usual
attention to detail, dates this with detailed accuracy
(vv.1-2). In modern language, we might call John a
public relations man. As he himself made very clear, his
one great task in life was to point people to Jesus (see
John 1.8 and 29-30). Three phrases help us to sum up
his ministry.

The Mission He Prized Elsewhere, the Bible tells us
that John was "a man sent from God" (John 1.6); here,
we are told that "the word of God came unto John" (v.2).
What is more, his ministry was itself the fulfilment of
prophecy (link vv.4-5 with Isaiah 40.3-4). There had not
been a prophet in the land for 400 years, but John was
the honoured successor of all those in the Old Testament. Later, Paul was to remind all Christians "We are
therefore Christ's ambassadors" (2 Corinthians 5.20
NIV), another honoured title carrying the same kind of
responsibility. How highly do you prize the position in
which God has placed you in the world? And how
seriously do you carry out your duties?

The Message He Preached In a nutshell, this was "a
baptism of repentance for the forgiveness of sins" (v.3
NIV), and when crowds flocked to be baptized (v.7)
John made it clear that repentance came first—he told

people "produce fruit in keeping with repentance" (v.8 NIV). He was more interested in examining hearts than in counting heads — a lesson for all Christian workers today! He then pressed home the urgency of his message by saying "the axe is already at the root of the trees" and that if there was no good fruit judgment would follow (v.9 NIV). When specific groups asked him how this life of repentance applied to them, his answers were clear and forthright. One group of people were told to be open-hearted and kind (v.11); the tax-collectors were to be scrupulously honest (v.13); the soldiers were to act with absolute integrity (v.14). Christians are expected to have the highest living standards in the world!

The Master He Proclaimed We have already seen that Isaiah's prophecy pin-pointed John's ministry as being "to prepare … the way of the Lord" (v.4) and when people were "waiting expectantly and were all wondering in their hearts if John might possibly be the Christ" (v.15 NIV) he made it quite clear that he was merely the forerunner of "one mightier than I" (v.16). *His* baptism would be "with the Holy Spirit and fire" (v.16 NIV). There may be a link here with Malachi 3.1-3, in which case the picture is that of the Holy Spirit purging and purifying the life of the Christian with the purpose of making him more and more like Christ. For those unwilling to submit to the fire of cleansing, there would one day be the fire of judgment (v.17). John's fearless preaching against the specific sins of Herod Antipas, the ruler of Galilee, eventually landed him in prison (vv.19-20) but he remained faithful to his commission— a P.R. man for Jesus!

"So do not be ashamed to testify about our Lord" (2 Timothy 1.8 NIV)

10
Just A List of Names?
Luke 3.21-38

In the passage covered by our last study, Luke brought us up-to-date with the story of John the Baptist, telling us of the beginning of his public ministry and then jumping ahead to tell us that he was eventually sent to prison for his outspoken denunciation of Herod's sins (vv.19-20). Now, Luke brings the real subject of his biography back into the picture (v.21). Matthew tells us that John was reluctant to baptize Jesus, but Jesus insisted that this was the right thing to do (see Matthew 3.14-15). Although without any sin of his own, Jesus identified himself with the sinners he came to save. The remarkable "appearance" of the Holy Spirit, and the audible voice from heaven, must have made this an astonishing moment for all who saw it! But most of today's reading is taken up with Jesus' genealogical table or family tree. Yet even this is part of God's Word, and therefore of value to us (see 2 Timothy 3.16). The list of names tells us three things about Jesus.

It Shows His Humanity The fact that Jesus *had* a family tree shows that he was not a figment of the imagination or a kind of mythological half-man-half-god. He was by turns a baby, a child, a teenager, and a mature man; he "grew in wisdom and statute" (Luke 2.52 NIV). He knew what it was to be hungry (Luke 4.2), thirsty (John 4.7) and tired (John 4.6). He was neither superman, supermyth, nor superstar. Jesus came to earth "in human likeness" (Philippians 2.7 NIV). One of the many great truths which follows is that he now intimately understands the problems and pressures that face us day by day. Hebrews 4.15 brings this out very well—and the next verse tells us what to do as a result.

It Supports His Authority The Jewish priests, called

Levites, began their public ministry "from thirty years old and upward" (see Numbers 4.47)—and Jesus chose the same moment to begin his (v.23). Yet if he was really the Messiah he would need to be able to prove his direct descent from King David (link Jeremiah 23.5 and 2 Samuel 7.12-13 with Acts 2.29-30 and Acts 13.22-23). Now notice how, even before his birth, the angel spoke of Jesus being given "the throne of His father David" (see 1.32). And here, in his family tree, the last name in verse 31 slots right into place! Even by "natural" means, the claims Jesus later made to be the Messiah had exactly the support they needed.

It Suggests His Divinity The final man mentioned in the family tree is Adam, and he is described as "the son of God". This would normally mean that Jesus was in a direct line of created descent—but notice how precisely this error is avoided. In verse 23 Luke speaks of Jesus "being *(as was supposed)* the son of Joseph". This was what people *thought* (look up Matthew 13.55, for instance) but they were mistaken. He was the son of Mary, but not of Joseph. The angel's message to Mary made it clear that the conception of Jesus in the womb would be the miraculous work of the Holy Spirit (see 1.35) and now, at the beginning of his public ministry, God announces him to be "my beloved Son" (v.22). The family tree suggests that Jesus was more than a mere man— the New Testament as a whole makes it clear that he was no less than God!

"…a descendant of David…declared with power to be the Son of God" (Romans 1.3-4 NIV).

11
Triumphant In Temptation
Luke 4.1-13

These opening verses of Luke 4 contain what must surely be one of the mot remarkable passages in the whole Bible. Although the language is very simple, and the whole section itself less than 200 words in length, it records a direct confrontation between Jesus and the devil. The subject of the whole passage is, of course, temptation, and because this is something so real to every Christian in the world, we should study these words with great care. One of the greatest lessons comes across in the opening verse, where we are told that Jesus was "full of the Holy Spirit" and that he was "led by the Spirit in the desert" (v.1 NIV). This shows us very clearly that when a person is severely tempted it does *not* mean that he is living a sub-standard life. Jesus was fiercely tempted throughout his earthly life, yet at no point was he less than perfect. Note Hebrews 4.15 very carefully. With that truth clearly in our minds we can now look in detail at the temptations Jesus faced at this particular point in his life.

They Were Diverse Notice how the devil switched his point of attack. Firstly, there were six weeks of unspecified but uninterrupted assaults (notice that at verse 2). Then the devil tried to capitalise on a physical weakness, the fact that Jesus was hungry (v.3). Next, he attempted the predictable avenue of pride (vv.5-7). Finally, he tempted Jesus to misuse his unique relationship to his heavenly Father, and though out of context, to stretch God's promises to cover personal folly (vv.9-11). In this third temptation the devil even had the audacity to quote the Bible (see Psalm 91.11-12). Let this be a lesson to us all! The devil has a thousand ways in which to attack the Christian, and he is capable of switching tactics with bewildering speed. Learn the discipline of being on your guard at all times. Matthew 26.41 contains the Christian-soldier's Orders for the Day!

They Were Deceptive Glance through these three temptations again and notice how *attractive* they all were. By yielding to the first, Jesus could have ended the pangs of hunger from which he was suffering. By yielding to the second, he could have set up an immediate earthly kingdom. By yielding to the third, he could have become a superstar overnight. But had he yielded at any of these points his whole life's mission would have collapsed. No wonder Paul speaks of "the strategies and the deceits of the devil" (Ephesians 6.11 AMP) and that Jesus warned us plainly that "when (the devil) lies, he speaks his native language…" (John 8.44 NIV). Temptation always promises more than it produces. There may be pleasure in sin, as Hebrews 11.25 admits quite openly, but there is never satisfaction. Study this whole subject carefully and aim to be able to say what Paul did at the end of 2 Corinthians 2.11!

They Were Defeated Surrounded as we are by temptations of every kind it is a great encouragement to read that when Jesus had firmly and successfully resisted all of these attacks, the devil "departed from him" (v.13). Even so, we must also note that he only went away "until another more opportune and favourable time" (v.13 AMP). In the same way, we dare not think that victory over one attack means immunity from any other. Notice, too, that the devil was defeated not by a histrionic display of supernatural power, but by a right use of scripture (look at vv. 4, 8 and 12) and because Jesus was filled with the Holy Spirit. He left the wilderness as he entered it, "in the power of the Spirit" (v.14). Victory over every temptation *is* possible, as 1 Corinthians 10.13 makes clear, but only in the combined power of the holy scriptures and the Holy Spirit.

"Submit yourselves therefore to God. Resist the devil and he will flee from you" (James 4.7)

12
The Voice of The People...
Luke 4.14-30

After the ordeal in the wilderness Jesus moved up country to Galilee (v.14) and settled for a while in his home town of Nazareth (v.16). In the course of today's reading Luke makes one brief comment on his ministry in general, and then gives us a more detailed description of one incident at Nazareth in particular. If we put these two sections of the narrative together, we can listen to the reaction of the people of his day to the life and teaching of Jesus.

Praise When Jesus began preaching in the local Galilean synagogues, news of his ministry "spread through the whole countryside" (v.14 NIV). Before long he was being "recognised and honoured and praised by all" (v.15 AMP). At this particular point in the story we are not given any specific details as to either the words or the actions which sparked off such enthusiasm, but it is surely not difficult to imagine the situation. He had come into Galilee "in the power of the Spirit" (v.14) and this must surely have meant that his dynamic ministry was in vivid contrast to a great deal of deadness among local congregations. Everybody who seeks to lead others in worship should constantly pray to be delivered from the dreadful drudgery of "services as usual" and to be liberated into the place where God speaks and people sit up and take notice. If only all today's preachers and teachers were able to say what Paul did at 1 Corinthians 2.4!

Prejudice It is important to notice in passing that Jesus was a regular worshipper in his local church (link v.16 with Hebrews 10.25). When on this particular occasion he got to his feet to read the scriptures, he was handed a scroll containing part of Isaiah's prophecy (v.17). He then read a brief passage (compare vv. 18-19 with Isaiah 61.1-2), rolled up the scroll and sat down (v.20). As this was the normal position for a preacher, "the eyes of everyone in the synagogue were fastened on him (v.20) — obviously waiting to hear what this remarkable man had to say. If they expected a sensation, they were not disappointed, because his opening words were "Today this scripture is fulfilled in your hearing" (v.21 NIV). In the plainest way he claimed to be the living fulfilment of Isaiah's ancient prophecy, in other words to be the Messiah. While the people were forced to admire his "gracious words", they could still only think of him as a young man from their own town (v.22). In a smaller way, we will sometimes face the same kind of prejudice, and this is especially likely to happen at home or at work. But in some cases, it will be because people do not like Christianity at close quarters!

Persecution Anticipating that they would ask for some startling proof of his claim (compare v.23 with Matthew 12.38 and 16.1) Jesus condemned their built-in prejudice with a proverb (v.24). He might have got away with that, but he then went on to give two Old Testament illustrations of Jews rejecting genuine prophets. In the first, Elijah was helped, not by Jews but by a foreigner from Zarephath in Sidon (link vv.25-26 with 1 Kings 17.1-9). In the second, there is no record of Elisha healing any of the "many lepers" in Israel, yet he gladly helped the Syrian army captain Naaman (link v.27 with 2 Kings 5.1-14). This triggered off a furious reaction, with the members of the congregation so enraged that they tried to throw him over a nearby cliff (v.29). But in a quiet display of magnificent authority he simply "walked right through the crowd and went on his way" (v.30 NIV). No Christian can avoid persecution of one kind or another — but 2 Corinthians 4.17-18 puts it all into perspective!

"...*everyone who wants to live a godly life in Christ Jesus will be persecuted*" (2 Timothy 3.12 NIV)

24

13
...And The Voice Of God
Luke 4.31-44

Moving on from Nazareth (which we never hear of him visiting again), Jesus went to Capernaum on the northern shore of the Sea of Galilee, and continued his preaching, including regular ministry in the synagogue throughout the whole area of Judea. (vv.31 and 44) Luke obviously condenses an extended period of ministry into a few verses, but this only serves to emphasise the fact that these days were packed with dynamic action. And it was not just action but *Divine* action. Luke is not just reporting the spectacular progression of an enthusiastic young preacher. Here is *God* on the loose, sweeping into one situation after another and transforming them through the words spoken by his Son. In our last study we heard the voice of the people — a disappointing mixture of praise, prejudice and persecution. In this passage we can listen to the voice of God, the impact of which can be summed up in four paragraphs.

Doctrine Was Revealed People were amazed at the teaching of Jesus, "for his word was with authority and ability and weight and power" (v.32 AMP). Religious teachers were two a penny at that time, but Jesus was different (see Matthew 7.29 for the way in which this contrast was expressed on another occasion). Others groped for the truth; Jesus revealed it, both in his words and in his life (see John 14.6). Titus 2.10 says something very significant to us in this whole area of the relationship between life and truth.

Demons Were Rebuked It is extraordinary to notice how the evil spirits recognised Jesus (vv.34 and 41)—a sobering reminder of their supernatural intelligence. Yet their knowledge produced only fear and terror (compare v.34 with James 2.19). With majestic authority Jesus rebuked them again and again (vv.35 and 41). Evil spirits are still actively at work today and demon possession is still a terrible reality, with appalling effects on individuals and society. But however terrifying the powers of evil may be, the Christian can rejoice in knowing that his Saviour and Lord is one whose superior authority is such that he is able to say "All power is given unto me in heaven and in earth" (Matthew 28.18). Make a careful note of how emphatically this same great truth is expressed at 1 Peter 3.22.

Disease Was Removed From the synagogue Jesus went to Simon Peter's house, where his mother-in-law was "suffering in the grip of a burning fever" (v.38 AMP). This is a vivid medical phrase—Colossians 4.14 tells us why Luke was qualified to use it. At the request of those present, Jesus rebuked the disease —just as he had the demons! — and her temperature quickly dropped to normal (v.39). All disease is primarily the result of sin— though not always *directly* so (see John 9.1-3) — and is therefore subordinate to the power of God. While God uses the body's natural mechanism, drugs, medicine and medical skill to restore people to health today, he also works directly and by miraculous means. Do we limit God by locking this kind of healing away within the covers of the Bible?

Duty Was Required It is lovely to notice that as soon as Peter's mother-in-law had been healed she started attending to the needs of others (v.39). Later, Jesus told those who wanted to detain him that he must go elsewhere to preach "the good news of the kingdom of God" (v.43 NIV). The fact that the Lord is King *is* good news—but it also demands obedience, duty and service. Paul called himself "a servant of God, and an apostle of Jesus Christ" (Titus 1.1). As a Christian, you share the same high privilege—and the same searching responsibility.

"O that today you would hearken to his voice" (Psalm 95.7 RSV)

14
Jesus Is Lord
Luke 5.1-16

Today's reading continues Luke's account of the public ministry of Jesus in the general area of Judea. The passage divides itself very clearly into two separate incidents, one by the "lake of Gennesaret", that is the Sea of Galilee (v.1) and the other in a unnamed town (v.12). Each of the incidents centres on a miracle performed by Jesus, the first demonstrating his mastery over nature and the second demonstrating his mastery over the human body. Later in the New Testament, we are shown that one of the earliest and simplest confessions of a Christian's faith was "Jesus is Lord" (Romans 10.9 NIV). That truth comes across loud and clear as we read this part of Luke's account of Christ's words and actions.

Unqualified Obedience The numbers of people following Jesus were growing all the time, and the chapter opens with "the people crowding around him and listening to the word of God" (v.1 NIV). Indeed, the crowds were so large that Jesus had to think of some means of ensuring that they could all see and hear him. Seeing two fishing-boats drawn up by the lake, he climbed into one of them (the one belonging to Simon Peter) and asked him to put out a little from the shore. The result was an ideal pulpit from which he was able to be seen and heard clearly (vv.2-3). When he had finished teaching the people, Jesus asked Peter to sail into deeper water in order to catch some fish (v.4). To an experienced Galilean fisherman, the idea was absurd. After all, they had worked hard all night and caught nothing (v.5). If the experts had drawn a blank during prime fishing time, what chance did they stand at the worst time of day? Yet Peter's doubts were immediately overtaken by his willingness to obey—*"Because you say so, I will let down the nets"* (v.5 NIV). Here is a vital principle for every Christian's life, because in practical terms, Christianity *is* obedience. Repentance, faith, prayer, witnessing, love, kindness, humility, holiness — all of these are commanded, and are therefore part of the believer's basic duty. The Bible's overall message to the Christian is Mary's word to the disciples at Cana — "Whatever he says to you, do it" (John 2.5 AMP). Are you being consciously obedient to all of God's revealed will to you? The outcome of Peter's obedience was amazing — his ship was filled with fish (v.7); his heart was filled with worship (v.8 and link this with Isaiah 6.5); and his life was filled with service! (v.11).

Unmerited Compassion In Bible times, sufferers from leprosy were literally avoided like the plague. They were forced to live in isolation while their bodies rotted away. Lepers were written off as unclean, defiled, unwanted. Yet when a man in an advanced state of the disease — we are told that he was "covered with leprosy" (v.12 NIV) — flung himself at the feet of Jesus and cried, "Lord, if you are willing, you can make me clean" (v.12 NIV) Jesus did both the unthinkable and the impossible: he *touched* him, and said "I am willing. Be clean!" (v.13 NIV). The man was healed immediately (v.13) and Jesus told him to fulfil the Old Testament requirement for obtaining a clean bill of health from the priest (link v.14 with Leviticus 14.7). This deeply moving incident is a beautiful illustration of Christ's mission in the world. Man is full of the leprosy of sin and (even worse than in the physical equivalent) he is fully deserving of the death it brings (Romans 5.12). Yet if he is willing to repent of his sin he will discover that Jesus is willing to touch him and heal him — notice how beautifully John 3.17 fits in with 2 Peter 3.9! As Christians, too, we need to open our lives in every part to the Lord's "I am willing", in order to be "filled with all the fulness of God" (Ephesians 3.19).

"His hands make whole" (Job 5.18)

15
Men Who Met The Master
Luke 5.17-39

In reading the Gospels we are, of course, reading the biography of Jesus and it is therefore to be expected that he holds the centre of the stage. But we can also learn a great deal by focussing some of our attention on the other people involved in the narrative as it unfolds. Their actions and attitudes can teach us a great deal, often by way of example or warning. Today's passage, which contains three separate incidents, is a good illustration of this.

The Man Who Was Cured By now, Jesus was mobbed wherever he went, people coming from miles around to listen to his teaching (v.17). In the middle of one indoor session, certain men (we are told at Mark 2.3 that there were four of them) brought a paralysed friend on his sleeping mat and tried to get him to Jesus. Unable to get through the crowd, they carried him up the outside steps to the flat roof, broke it open and let the sick man down through the hole they had made (v.19). Jesus' immediate response was not to heal him, but to forgive him (v.20), an action which immediately caused the scribes and Pharisees to level a charge of blasphemy at him for claiming to do something that was God's prerogative (v.21). In reply, Jesus asked them a question: did they think it easier to pronounce words of forgiveness or of healing? (v.23) The point behind the question is that the first would seem to be easier, because the other would need an obvious miracle to prove that the words had been effective. Without waiting for their answer, Jesus proceeded to add the "difficult" word (v.24) and the man was cured in an instant (v.25) with the result that "everyone was amazed and gave praise to God" (v.26 NIV). But notice one very important phrase — Jesus acted "when he saw their faith" (v.20). The whole incident hinges on this. Are you proving promises like the one at Matthew 17.20...or praying along the lines of Luke 17.5?

The Man Who Was Called Levi (also known as Matthew — see Matthew 9.9) was a civil servant working in the local tax office (v.27). When Jesus said to him "Follow me" (v.27) his response was immediate and wholehearted (v.28). What is more, he arranged an evangelistic dinner (that same night?) inviting many of his unconverted colleagues and friends to meet Jesus (v.29). The religious diehards did not approve of a religious teacher mixing with outsiders, but Jesus put them neatly in their place with two unanswerable comments (vv.31-32). The obvious challenge of Matthew's call is one of happy boldness in sharing his faith with others. An Old Testament prophet had caught the same spirit (see Isaiah 63.7). Have you?

The Men Who Were Confused Some people were puzzled as to why the followers of Jesus did not make fasting part of their religion, as did the followers of John the Baptist (v.33). In reply, Jesus said that wedding guests did not fast in the bridegroom's presence (v.34) — notice that John the Baptist used the same joyful picture of his relationship to Jesus (John 3.29). He then gave a veiled prophecy of his death, after which fasting would be appropriate (v.35). The two tiny parables that followed (vv. 36-39) both pointed out the same truth — the Christian life is exhilarating and dynamic, and cannot be contained in worn-out structures. The lesson for us is that we should let our approach to Christian life and witness be as fresh as the Christian message itself. Romans 14.17 will help!

"We have seen the Lord" (John 20.25)

16
The Lord!
Luke 6.1-16

As Jesus continued his ministry, the Pharisees, a strictly orthodox Jewish sect, continued to find fault with the way he did things. As we shall see several times in these studies, his behaviour on the Sabbath was a particularly frequent bone of contention. In this passage he deals with two criticisms levelled at him, and chooses twelve apostles—and in doing so shows himself to be the Lord.

Lord Of The Sabbath The disciples' actions in verse 1 seem harmless enough to us, but they were not to the Pharisees. This particular interpretation of religious laws was so detailed and absurd that plucking corn was equivalent to reaping; rubbing the corn in the hand was threshing; picking out the kernels from the husks (which the disciples must have done before eating them) was winnowing; and the whole process meant that they had in effect engaged in the work of preparing food for eating. This was their line of thinking, and it meant that in their eyes the disciples were religious criminals engaged in wholesale law-breaking. Such blatant wickedness could not go unchallenged, so they bluntly demanded "why are you doing what is unlawful on the Sabbath?" (v.2 NIV). In reply, Jesus quoted an Old Testament incident—link vv.3-4 with 1 Samuel 21.1-6—in which David (one of their great heroes) and his men had once asked for, and been given by the priest, bread solemnly set aside for the priests' exclusive use in accordance with Leviticus 24.5-9. The inference was that if David's need took preference over established ceremonial law, the disciples' hunger (see Matthew 12.1) must surely take precedence over the Pharisees' ridiculous interpretation of the law of Moses. What is more, Jesus went on to claim that he was "Lord of the Sabbath" (v.5), with the obvious inference that he was not subject to any man-made additions to the Divine law. On another Sabbath, Jesus was confronted in the synagogue by a man with a withered hand (v.6). Notice that the careful Dr. Luke even tells us which hand it was! Sensing that Jesus might take action to heal the man, the Pharisees were ready to pounce again (v. 7). But Jesus forestalled them with an unanswerable question (v.9) which again appealed to mercy as a law which should come first — see what he calls it in Matthew 23.23. Getting no answer, Jesus promptly healed the man (v.10) — but the Pharisees were so bigoted that they raged when they should have rejoiced (v.11). Binding these two incidents together is that tremendous statement we saw in verse 5 — "The Son of Man is Lord of the Sabbath". This was an electrifying claim! After all, the Sabbath was instituted by God (Exodus 20.8-11); for Jesus to claim authority over it could mean only one thing!

Lord Of The Harvest Twelve ordinary men were now to play an important role in the ministry of Jesus, both in terms of fellowship and service (notice these in Mark 3.14-15). They were chosen out of many disciples (the word means "learners") to be apostles (meaning "special messengers"). But the really instructive thing is to notice what Jesus did immediately *before* he chose them (v.12). Now link this up with what he said in Matthew 9.37-38. Prayer is not just *part* of our responsibility in Christian service; it is the *first* part. We need to pray for discernment, directions, and the dynamic of all we seek to do for the Lord of the harvest. The alternative is to find John 15.5 illustrated as in Luke 5.5!

"You call me 'Teacher' and 'Lord', and rightly so, for that is what I am" (*John 13.13 NIV*).

17
The Sermon On The Plain (1)
Luke 6.17-36

At this point in our studies in the biography of Jesus we come to one of the occasions when Luke records for us notes of one of the sermons which Jesus preached. It is sometimes thought that this sermon is merely another version of what we call The Sermon on the Mount, which is recorded at Matthew 5, 6 and 7, but it is perhaps more likely that the sermon reported by Luke was given on a quite different occasion, though it did contain a number of similar sayings. One of the obvious differences in the two narratives is in the wording of the introductions to the sermons. Matthew says that Jesus "went up into a mountain" (Matthew 5.1) whereas Luke says that Jesus "went down with them and stood on a level place" (v.17 NIV) — though this could have been somewhere on a mountainside (see v.12). Needless to say, the context of the sermon in no way affects its content!

Life At Its Best The sermon begins at verse 20 with a series of "blessings" or as we sometimes call them, "beatitudes", changing at verse 24 to a series of "woes". Taken together, they form a collection of moral and spiritual bombshells because they are so revolutionary, because they challenged so many of the accepted teachings of the time. To summarize the first list, Jesus promised God's blessing on groups of people: firstly, on those who did not trust in themselves (compare v.20 with Matthew 5.3 which brings out the meaning more clearly); secondly, on those who were spiritually hungry (compare v.21 with Matthew 5.6 which explains the kind of hunger Jesus meant); thirdly, on those who mourned over sin, and especially their own sin (compare v.21 with Matthew 5.4); and fourthly on those who suffered for the sake of their Christian faith and life (compare vv.22-23 with Matthew 5.10-12). In these few verses we are given God's blueprint for blessing. To what extent are you following the Divine pattern? The "woes" are addressed to the self-reliant, who go through life well off (v.24), well fed (v.25) well satisfied (v.25) and well thought of (v.26), and yet without a living faith in God (which is the inference we are meant to draw). Jesus was not suggesting that money, food, happiness and popularity were in any way wrong, but that they were *insufficient*. Although it is temporary, life must be seen in the light of eternity, and life at its best means putting God first, even when these apparently attractive things do not even come second! For the Christian, the guidelines are laid down in Colossians 3.1-2.

Love At Its Best It would not be an over-simplification to say that Christian love is Christian faith in action, and Jesus now went on to take this love to its ultimate expression. The teaching of verses 27-36 could be summarized in one simple but stupendous phrase — "Love your enemies" (vv. 27 and 35). The Jews already knew the Old Testament command "Love your neighbour" (Leviticus 19.18), but many accepted the false corollary that they could therefore hate their enemies (Jesus quoted this in Matthew 5.43). Jesus now completely destroyed that false argument. As it is perfectly obvious that God pours out certain blessings even on those who openly disobey him, Christians should love their enemies and thus prove their own relationship to God (notice how this is put at v.35). This particular section of the sermon is summed up in what is sometimes called The Golden Rule — "Do to others as you would have them do to you" (v.31 NIV). To follow that rule will be to guarantee warm-hearted, generous, thoughtful, sacrificial kindness — and that is love at its best!

"...let us not love with words or tongue but with actions and in truth" (1 John 3.18 NIV).

34

18
The Sermon On The Plain (2)
Luke 6.37-49

The Jews had a word for a certain kind of preaching which we could literally translate as "stringing beads together". We have a good example of this in this particular passage, because in these thirteen verses, which can be read in about two minutes, Jesus touched on at least six different subjects.

Criticism (v.37) The promises contained in the three maxims Jesus lay down here are true both on earth and in heaven. The man who is harsh and critical in his treatment of others will surely find those people behaving in exactly the same way towards him. But what is even more serious is that such an attitude on his part proves that he does not have the love of God in his heart. (By contrast notice what Paul says about the spiritual man at Romans 5.5.) And the man without the love of God in his heart is clearly unsaved.

Generosity (v.38) Here is another law which can be applied in two ways, practically and spiritually. On a human level, generosity tends to be contagious or at the least reciprocal — even among unconverted men! — as Jesus pointed out at verse 33. Beyond that, God promises direct reward to those who are generous to others. Notice how Paul puts this in Philippians 4.18-19!

Spiritual Vision (vv. 39-40) Many of those who heard Jesus were not only learners, they would one day be leaders. It was therefore vital that they should know what they were teaching and where they were going. Notice how Jesus applied this to the Pharisees in Matthew 15.12-14. It is surely stating the obvious to say that no man can lead another to a place without first getting there himself. Spiritually, this demands great discipline and self-examination on the part of the Christian. James 3.1 warns of the presumption of thinking otherwise!

Hypocrisy (vv.41-42) To illustrate this, Jesus uses the superb hyperbole of a man with a plank of wood jutting out of his eye while he tries to remove a tiny speck of sawdust from his brother's eye (v.42). It is easy to laugh at the picture — but not so easy to obey the lesson it teaches. Before you criticise others, be sure that you are not at fault in that area. If you feel you must concern yourself with the failings of others, make sure that you read Galatians 6.1 first!

Words and Actions (vv.43-45) The truths of vv.43-44 are obvious; and the application is equally plain, as Jesus pointed out in Matthew 7.15-20. A man's actions do not so much *make* his character as *reveal* it — and so do his words! (v.45) Jesus himself was a perfect example of this (look back at 4.22). The exhortation in Hebrews 13.15 links fruit and speech neatly together!

Obedience (vv. 46-49) The point of this well-known parable is often missed. The foundation that Jesus commends is not mere knowledge (both men had that —see vv.47 and 49) but *obedience*. It is only when we add the discipline of obedience (the building, digging and laying of v.48) to the raw materials of truth that we will have a foundation that will stand the test of life. Obedience helps to build moral fibre; casual hearing gives a man no defence when trouble comes.

"Be ... doers of the word, and not hearers only" (James 1.22)

19

"He Healed The Sick And Raised The Dead..."

Luke 7.1-17

"...Yes, he did!", the song goes on, and in today's reading we have an illustration of each of these remarkable miracles. From the detailed narratives, two features stand out vividly.

A Soldier's Faith The centurion (v.1) was a high-ranking Roman soldier. From Luke's account of this particular incident, we can pull together some interesting threads of truth about his character. For instance, we know that he was kind; although slaves were usually treated like pieces of furniture, this man had one "who was held in honour and highly valued by him" (v.2 AMP). Then, we know that he was tolerant: Jews and Gentiles usually mixed like mercury and water!—notice what is said at John 4.9—yet the Jews were able to tell Jesus "This man...loves our nation" (vv.4-5 NIV). Next, the Jews made it clear that he was religiously inclined: not only had he shown an overall respect for them, but, in their own words, he had "built us our synagogue at his own expense" (v.5 AMP). He was also remarkably humble: while his Jewish friends commended him to Jesus as being "worthy" (v.4), he took exactly the opposite line, and protested that he was "not worthy", either for Jesus to enter his house, nor for he himself to come near to Jesus (compare vv.6-7 with the attitude adopted by the tax collector at Luke 18.13). But a further quality outshone even these—and that was his astonishing faith in the healing power of Jesus. He was apparently quite convinced that all Jesus had to do was to "say the word" and the slave would recover (v.7 NIV). Jesus was so impressed with this that he ranked it as greater than any degree of faith he had ever found, even among the Jews (v.9). The centurion's reward matched his faith perfectly, for when the servants returned to the house they "found the servant well" (v.10 NIV). This unnamed Roman soldier—perhaps not even a true disciple at this point—stands as a challenge to every Christian, and as a rebuke to most. So many Christians badly need a faith lift! Defective faith results in aimlessness (Proverbs 3.5-6), uncertainty (2 Chronicles 20.20) and spiritual injury (Ephesians 6.16). The gift and the exercise of faith are absolutely essential for healthy growth in the Christian life.

The Saviour's Love The next miracle took place just outside the Galilean town of Nain (v.11). Luke is the only New Testament writer to record the incident, and he does so with artless simplicity and stunning effect. A widow's only son was being carried to the cemetery, accompanied by a large crowd of mourners (v.12). In what may have been very little more time than it takes to tell, Jesus comforted the widow (v.13), halted the procession and commanded the corpse to come back to life (v.14). With a perfect economy of words, Luke goes on "The dead man sat up and began to talk" (v.15 NIV). The reaction recorded in vv.16-17 is hardly surprising! There was little doubt in the minds of the people that they had seen God at work in their midst that day. Yet the loveliest thing in this incident is that we are told "When Jesus saw her, *his heart went out to her*" (v.13 NIV). His heart went out before either his hand or his word! The love of Jesus surges through the whole of the New Testament—John 13.1, Romans 8.35-39 and Galatians 2.20 are but a few examples. Should this not have a decisive effect on our faith?

"I do believe; help me overcome my unbelief!" (Mark 9.24 NIV)

20
Jesus and John
Luke 7.18-35

John the Baptist comes briefly back into the picture at this stage. He was in prison at the time (the reason is given in Matthew 14.3-4) but visiting friends had told him about the astonishing things Jesus was doing (v.18). The message he sent to Jesus leads us into today's reading.

An Anxious Request On the face of it, it seems strange that the question in vv.19-20 should be asked by the one who had confidently identified Jesus with the words "Behold, the Lamb of God, who takes away the sin of the world!" (John 1.29) Was he becoming impatient for Jesus to take some political action to overthrow the Romans? Was his faith beginning to erode? Was the question being asked, not for John's own benefit, but on behalf of his disciples? Was he wondering why Jesus did not mount some spectacular rescue mission to get him out of prison? Or were the reports he was getting so garbled that he wanted more evidence? We are not told —but the very fact that the question was asked is helpful to us. It shows that in spite of the tremendous impact he made on his generation John, like his great Old Testament counterpart Elijah, was "a man just like us" (James 5.17 NIV). He knew what it was to be anxious, unsure and limited.

An Ample Reply If lack of evidence prompted the question, Jesus quickly supplied the answer (v.22). Who could dispute the claims of a man who did these things? It tied in exactly with the prophecy by Isaiah, that had been read by Jesus in the synagogue at Nazareth (look back to 4.18-19). In witness to others, learn to concentrate on the person and work of the Lord Jesus Christ. People must be brought face to face with *him*. Notice how the other John brings out the importance of what Jesus did — John 2.11; 3.2; 7.31; 10.25, 38; 20.30-31. Christianity is not based on philosophy, but on facts! Jesus then took the opportunity of commending John. He was not a fickle weakling — "a reed shaken with the wind" (v.24), nor an effeminate courtier — "a man dressed in fine clothes" (v.25 NIV). Jesus identified him as a prophet who had been prophesied! (see Malachi 3.1 and 4.5). What is more, he stood at the pinnacle of the prophets, the last (and in that sense the most important) of the line (v.28). Yet now, with the coming of Jesus, a new era had dawned, and even the most insignificant Christian possessed greater privileges and blessings than John (v.28). Do we fully realise that? Have we begun to grasp what is meant by 1 Corinthians 3.21-23?

An Angry Rebuke Jesus then turned from commending John to rebuking some of his hearers. Some acknowledged the truth of John's teaching and had in fact been baptized by him (v.29) but others had rejected both John and Jesus (v.30). They rejected John because they thought he was so austere that he must have been devil-possessed (v.33); and they rejected Jesus because they thought he was not austere enough (v.34). There was no pleasing them. They were like groups of fractious, restless children, unwilling to play either weddings or funerals! (vv. 31-32) However, the changed lives of God's people prove the wisdom of his ways (v.35). Beware of negative, barren criticism of other Christians just because they do things differently from you. Character is more important than life-style! John 21.20-22 are worth reading here!

"(The Lord) loves him who pursues righteousness" (Proverbs 15.9 RSV)

21
The Fruit Of Forgiveness
Luke 7.36-50

This incident took place at a dinner party in the house of a well-to-do Pharisee by the name of Simon (vv.36 and 40). The theme of the story as Luke tells it is forgiveness and from his fascinating narrative three things stand out.

Forgiveness Indicated Mingling with the guests (perhaps on the fringe of the crowd) was a woman with a notorious reputation for living "a sinful life" (v.37 NIV). But (so recently that the guests had not even heard of it?) something had happened to her. At one stage Jesus told his host "her many sins *have been* forgiven" (v.47 NIV) — and she must therefore have repented and changed her ways (notice the order of these words at 24.47). This may explain the boldness of her actions. As the guests reclined at table (they would have done this by leaning on one elbow, with their feet stretched out behind them) she suddenly began to weep. As her tears fell on Jesus' feet, she knelt down, wiped them with her hair, and "kissed his feet affectionately" (v.38 AMP). Then she anointed his feet with perfume from an alabaster (and therefore expensive) jar (v.39). As we see later, this seemingly extravagant demonstration of love was the result of her deep sense of gratitude. The first part of v.47 could be paraphrased "She has shown this amount of love because she has been forgiven so much sin". Is your love for Christ any indication of his love for you?

Forgiveness Illustrated When Simon saw what had happened, he thought that Jesus did not realise who the woman was — and that he could not, therefore, be a prophet sent from God (v.39). Although Simon had not said a word, we read that Jesus "answered him" (v.40).

He had not read Jesus' mind correctly—but Jesus had read his! The story Jesus told was perfectly straightforward (vv.41-42). One man owed a certain money-lender "five hundred pence" (about 18 months' wages); another owed him "fifty pence" (about two months' wages). As they were both bankrupt, he cancelled both debts. We shall see the application of the story in a moment—but notice that this is a perfect illustration of forgiveness. It is a cancellation of the debt of disobedience. This is brought out in Matthew's version of the Lord's Prayer (Matthew 6.12). On the basis of 1 Chronicles 16.29, how often do we need to be forgiven?

Forgiveness Demonstrated When Jesus asked Simon which of the two debtors would love their benefactor the most, he quickly gave the right answer (v.43). Jesus agreed—but then came the crunch! Simon, as the host that evening, had not even performed the common courtesies of the time towards him. He had given him neither water to rinse his feet (see Genesis 18.4); the customary kiss of welcome (see Romans 16.16); nor the normal touch of perfumed oil on the head (see Psalm 23.5). On the other hand, the uninvited stranger had lavished tears, kisses and perfume on him. The lesson was clear: much love was a sign of much forgiveness, and little love was a sign of little forgiveness (v.47). Simon's actions (or lack of them) had betrayed the state of his heart! To the amazement of the guests (link v.49 with Luke 5.21) Jesus publicly announced her forgiveness (v.48) and commended her faith (v.50). Contemplating Calvary is the greatest possible motivation of holy living and faithful service (see 2 Corinthians 5.14-15).

"We love him because he first loved us" (1 John 4.19)

22

The Purposes Of
The Parables

Luke 8.1-15

A parable has been described as "an earthly story with a heavenly meaning". Literally, the word means "to put things side by side in order to compare them". In the case of the parables of Jesus those two "things" were a short story and one particular spiritual truth, usually concerning the kingdom of God (v.10). The New Testament contains nearly 40 of the parables of Jesus, and at one stage we even read that "he did not say anything to them without using a parable" (Matthew 13.34 NIV). But if the parables of Jesus were so prominent, what was their purpose? There are two answers to that question, both of which can be seen in this particular passage.

To Reveal The Truth To Some Jesus made it clear that the meaning of this parable had to do with the way people listened to, or received "the word of God" (v.11). You can trace this in each part of his explanation of the story — he mentions "the ones who hear" (v.12 NIV); "the ones who receive the word" (v.13 NIV); "those who hear" (v.14 NIV); and "those...who hear the word" (v.15 NIV). In fact, when Jesus had told the parable to the crowds he added "He who has ears to hear, let him hear" (v.8 NIV). But notice what happened next. The disciples asked him what the parable meant (v.9). They were not satisfied with hearing a fascinating story and then indulging in idle speculation as to what it might mean. They wanted to *know,* and they came to the Lord for the answer. That must always be our attitude when reading the Bible. We can never understand it by mere human reasoning. But the Christian has two priceless assets. One is the Holy Spirit, who, it is promised, will lead him to know the truth (notice what Jesus said at John 16.13).

43

The other is prayer; surely the words of James 1.5 apply here? Notice too how Jesus emphasised that spiritual understanding is a gift from God (see the beginning of v.10). Spiritual truths are "mysteries" and only God can open them up to us. Get a grip on this—and learn to be grateful when God enables you to "see" what the Bible means. Matthew 11.25 will help to keep your gratitude humble!

To Conceal The Truth From Others However harsh this may seem, we must not run away from this very important point. Notice how it is made in the parable itself. People who hear the word casually, carelessly or superficially are like seed falling on a well-trodden path (compare v.5 with v.12), or on "rock" (compare v.6 with v.13), or among "thorns" (compare v.7 with v.14) — all failing to come to fruition. The whole point is devastatingly crystallised in the second part of v.10 (compare it with Psalm 78.2 and Isaiah 6.9-10). Those who treat parables as no more than interesting stories will end up with nothing but interesting stories! In spiritual matters, the clarity of men's hearing depends on the state of their hearts. Elsewhere, Jesus went even further and said that a man must be willing to *do* God's will before he will be able to *discern* it (see John 7.17). The man who is not prepared to *heed* the word of God will not even be able to *hear* it correctly! It is for this reason that the parables become *windows* to some people and *walls* to others. Learn to come to the Bible with an honest, open, earnest heart, genuinely willing to know and to do God's will. As you do, you will find yourself in the fruitful field of verse 15!

"If you cry out for insight ... then you will understand" (Proverbs 2.3-5 RSV)

23
Living The Christian Life
Luke 8.16-25

Not for the first time, our day's reading covers several apparently unconnected paragraphs, in this case three of them. Even if they were totally unrelated, they would not, of course, lose any of their authority, as they would still be part of God's Word. Taken together, however, they focus attention on three facets of living the Christian life.

Responsibility (vv.16-18) The command to "consider carefully how you listen" (v.18 NIV) links this first paragraph with the parable of the sower (look back at v.8) and reminds us of the responsibility of being an attentive *hearer* of God's Word. But we are also to be *doers,* and "not hearers only" (James 1.22)—and the two are vitally connected! Seed will bear fruit and a candle will light up a room *if put in the right place* — the Psalmist tells us of one very important responsibility in this area (Psalm 119.11). But there is another sense in which it must never be hidden (v.16). Jesus makes our responsibility even more solemn by reminding us that at the end of the day secrecy is impossible (link v.17 with 2 Corinthians 5.10). To all of this Jesus added a word of encouragement and a word of warning (v.18). One of God's spiritual laws could be summed up in the words "use or lose" (see the Parable of the Talents, for instance, at Matthew 25.14-30, and especially the last two verses).

Obedience (vv.19-21) The themes of hearing and obeying God's Word are repeated yet again at the end of this incident. The people who made the very ordinary comment at v.20 could hardly have expected the reply they received! (v.21) — which incidentally contains one of the Bible's loveliest descriptions of the relationship between Christians and the Lord Jesus. True believers are not seen by Jesus as mere slaves, but as friends (see John 15.15) and, even closer than that, as members of his family. If you look up Romans 8.17 you will see that this has relevance for the future as well as for the present! But notice, by linking v.21 with John 15.14 and 1 John 3.14, how the reality of that relationship can be tested. Are you developing the family likeness, and deepening the family love? These are the marks of *true* Christianity — see John 13.35.

Faith (vv.22-24) Weary after his long exertions, Jesus obviously wanted to cross the Sea of Galilee for a break from the demanding crowds. As he slept, a sudden storm swept down from the hills (v.23). Galilee is over 600 feet below sea level, and cool evening air rushing down the ravines in the hills produces exactly this result. Frightened out of their wits, and believing that they were going to be drowned, the disciples cried to Jesus for help (v.24). Waking up, he rebuked the wind and the waves, and in an instant the storm was over (v.24). On a previous occasion, Jesus had "rebuked" the fever gripping Peter's mother-in-law (see 4.39). Disease in the body and disorder in the natural world are ultimately (but not always directly) the result of sin's entry into the world; and these two incidents are vivid demonstrations of Christ's authority in both spheres! Finally, there was a rebuke (though of a different kind for the disciples—) "Where is your faith?" (v.25). They had been so frightened by the power of the wind that they had forgotten the greater power of the Lord. The Christian life is certainly not without its storms, but the Christian is never without a Saviour, and when he takes over there is always "a great calm" (Matthew 8.26). Incidentally, the answer to the disciples' question (v.25) is in Psalm 89.8-9!

"Submit ... to God; ... resist the devil" (James 4.7)

24
The Divine Exorcist
Luke 8.26-40

There is worldwide interest in the activities of evil spirits, and a great deal of discussion on how they can be dealt with. This passage shows us that neither the problem nor the solution are in any way new. In today's study we shall basically look at three phases of a remarkable incident which Luke describes.

Diagnosis As Jesus stepped ashore he was met by a man in a desperate condition. He was demon-possessed, naked, and lived among the dead in the local cemetery (v.27). Luke not only identifies an "unclean spirit" (v.29), but "many devils" (v.30) who had taken possession of the man. Yet perhaps nothing gives clearer evidence of the supernatural power of evil spirits than the diagnosis *they* made!—compare v.28 with Matthew 8.29 and Mark 5.7. No mere madman would have that kind of knowledge. It is staggering to realise that evil spirits recognised Jesus when most of the people did not! — and that they did so long before even someone like Peter made his great declaration of faith (see 9.20). In that sense, faith is not confined to Christians, nor even to men at large—see James 2.19. Never underestimate the reality or the ability of what Paul calls "the rulers of the darkness of this world" (Ephesians 6.12). Our attitude in this particular area is laid down for us very clearly in Deuteronomy 18.10-14.

Direction All attempts at taming this frightening, wild man had failed (v.29). There was no natural solution to a supernatural problem. The evil spirits instantly recognised that in Jesus they were faced with One who had authority over them—notice that they pleaded with him not to "order" them "to go into the Abyss" (v.31 NIV). This is a reference to the "bottomless pit" to which Satan and all his hosts will eventually be condemned (see Revelation 9.1, 11.7 and 20.1-15). Instead, they asked to be allowed to enter a herd of swine (v.32)—possibly in a frantic attempt to stave off or delay their inevitable doom? Given permission, they entered the pigs (there were about 2,000 of them — see Mark 5.13), at which "the herd rushed down the steep bank into the lake and was drowned (v.33 NIV). Why did Jesus allow this loss of livestock? The best answer would seem to be that he did so to help the man to *see* that his terrible ordeal was over. One man's health and sanity were more important than the lives of 2,000 animals. Man has been given God's authority to kill animals to supply his need for food; surely the Lord had authority to use them to supply a man's need of faith? But the key point here is that the only ultimate answer to demon possession was demon expulsion; and what was true then was true in the New Testament after Jesus' ascension (see Acts 8.7 for instance) and remains true today.

Deliverance The effect on the man was remarkable. People who came to see what had happened found him "clothed, and in his right mind" (v.35). Rid of the evil spirits, he was socially, morally and mentally re-integrated. All of this is in turn a picture of the truth that Jesus makes men "whole"; the Bible says that it is only "in him" that men are "complete" (Colossians 2.10). When the healed man asked if he might travel with him, Jesus refused his request, and instead commanded him to return to his own neighbours and tell them what God had done for him (v.39). Every Christian has the same responsibility. Are you seriously seeking to carry it out in the situation in which God has placed you?

"My mouth shall speak the praise of the Lord" (Psalm 145.21)

25
Faith Works!
Luke 8.41-56

Today's reading weaves together incidents concerning two very different people who both experienced the miraculous, healing touch of the Lord Jesus Christ; what links the two stories together is the great faith of the people involved in them.

Dying ... The passage opens with a man called Jairus coming to Jesus in great distress because his 12 year old daughter lay dying (vv.41-42). Although he was "a ruler of the synagogue", and therefore a leading figure in the religious community, notice that in his hour of need he "fell down at Jesus' feet" (v.41). Real faith always goes hand in hand with genuine humility. The Bible gives a solemn warning and a wonderful promise when it says that "God opposes the proud but gives grace to the humble" (1 Peter 5.5 NIV). Whenever you begin to feel self-sufficient, you will cease to ask God for his help; and when you cease to ask you cease to receive (check this with the end of James 4.2). In the case of Jairus, humility was married to extraordinary faith — Mark tells us that he asked Jesus, "Please come and put your hands on her so that she will be healed and live" (Mark 5.23 NIV).

...Dying... As Jesus started out for the home of Jairus, a woman who had been suffering from an incurable haemorrhage for 12 years "touched the border of his garment" (v.44). As we are told elsewhere, she was convinced that "If I just touch his clothes, I will be healed" (Mark 5.28 NIV). This showed amazing faith, in that no similar thing is recorded as having happened before! Her faith was rewarded instantly (v.44) but it brought a puzzling question from Jesus (v.45). When Peter pointed out that many people had been pressing against him (v.45) Jesus insisted that following one person's touch power had gone out of him (v.46). Realising that she could not escape attention, the woman, although terrified, owned up (v.47). She was immediately comforted by Jesus with the words "Your faith has healed you" (v.48 NIV). But why did Jesus insist on identifying her? According to laws laid down in Leviticus 15 (see from v.25 onwards), a woman in her condition was ceremonially unclean, and contaminated anyone she touched. It was therefore very important that everyone should know of her cure, so that she could return to normal life. What marvellous understanding Jesus showed!—and what a reminder to us that though sometimes hard, obedience is always rewarded (see Exodus 19.5).

...Dead! While this was happening, Jairus's daughter had died, and her father's request now seemed pointless (v.49). Yet Jesus told him that he must still have faith; his daughter would be restored (v.50). Arriving at the house he found it already filled with the usual professional mourning-party (including musicians! — see Matthew 9.23). When he told them to stop wailing, because the girl was only asleep, they "laughed him to scorn" because they knew perfectly well that she was dead (v.53). But Jesus was using the same kind of language as he did concerning Lazarus (see John 11.11-14). The reality of her death is shown by the words describing the miracle that followed, "her spirit returned" (v.55 NIV). The lovely touch at the end of v.55 reminds us that Jesus is as concerned about the ordinary provision of meals as the extraordinary performance of miracles! Matthew 6.25-34 is the perfect passage about this—and is in turn a direct challenge to exercise daily faith in God for the provision of the little as well as the large things of life.

"Have faith in God" (Mark 11.22)

26
Enough For Every Need
Luke 9.1-17

As with yesterday's reading, we have two separate incidents here, linked by one common feature, in this case the Lord's ability to supply all people's needs, whatever their circumstances.

The Sending of The Messengers The first thing mentioned in this chapter needs to be seen in the light of the fact that the life of Jesus was approaching a critical phase. His ministry in Galilee would soon be over (look ahead to what is said at v.51) and popularity would soon be replaced by opposition. Jesus therefore made specific plans to send the disciples out to make a final concentrated effort in the area (v.1). Although Luke does not mention the fact, it is interesting to notice that they went out in six teams of two (see Mark 6.7). Luke does, however, tell us three very important things about the ministry of these men. Firstly, it was a *delegated* ministry. The "power and authority" they had was not their own (v.1), nor was the kingdom they were to preach! (v.2). In all your Christian work, remember who is the Lord and who are the labourers (see 10.2). Then it was a *definite* ministry—they were to "preach the kingdom of God and heal the sick" (v.2). Their business was not political propaganda nor moral platitudes. Instead, they were to minister in God's name to men's spiritual and physical needs. The miracles would have underlined their doctrine in a most powerful way. Finally, it was a *dependent* ministry. Look at v.3. The "scrip" may have been the equivalent of a begging-bowl, which was used by some itinerant preachers at that time. But whatever the precise detail, the principle was clear: they were to travel light, depending on God to provide food, shelter and clothing as they were needed. It all sounds pretty hazardous, but you can check at 22.35 as to whether it worked out! God never calls a man to do a work for him without guaranteeing his lines of supply— and sometimes he asks a man to start with no resources in sight. But this is not always the case — see 22.36.

The Feeding of The Multitude This is one of the best-known stories in the New Testament, recorded in all four Gospels. When they returned from their extraordinary mission, Jesus held a de-briefing session with the disciples and then took them by boat (see Mark 6.32) for rest and relaxation (v.10). Time spent quietly alone with Jesus is never time wasted. But soon they were thronged again (compare v.11 with Mark 6.33-34) and Jesus immediately began preaching and healing those who were sick (v.11). As evening drew on, the disciples asked him to send the people away for food and lodging (v.12). When Jesus (with a smile?) suggested that they feed them, the disciples replied that there was hardly any food available—just five loaves and two fish belonging to a small boy—compare v.15 with John 6.8. Although there were over 5,000 people in the crowd (read v.14 with Matthew 14.21) Jesus ordered them to sit down in groups of fifty (vv.14-15). He then "gave thanks" (v.16 NIV) and asked the disciples to begin passing the food to the people. Amazingly, it never ran out, everybody had enough to eat and even the crumbs filled twelve baskets (v.17). There have been attempts to explain away this miracle — but in the light of Psalm 33.6 and John 1.3 this is totally unnecessary! Finally, notice the link with yesterday's reading about faith. Then look up Psalm 37.25, and ask yourself whether your attitude to life reflects the truth of David's testimony.

"My God shall supply all your need" (Philippians 4.19)

27
The Cross and The Crown
Luke 9.18-36

As we saw yesterday, our studies have reached a turning-point in the earthly life of Jesus. He now felt that it was time to assess the response to his ministry. The question in verse 18 brought an extraordinary answer (v.19). Many people thought that Jesus was a re-incarnation of John the Baptist; others thought that he was the prophet Elijah (with whose teaching that of John the Baptist had already been linked — see 1.17); while others thought that he was another of the prophets come back to life. Jesus immediately made it clear that the issue must be taken further; the inescapable question was "Who do *you* say I am?" (v.20 NIV). Christianity is concerned with the person of Christ as well as with his works, and it demands an individual response, not merely knowledge of other people's opinions. Peter's answer (compare v.20 with the fuller rendering at Matthew 16.16) marks one of the most electrifying moments in the New Testament. "Christ" is the equivalent of "Messiah", the promised Deliverer for whom the Jews were longing. To avoid the impression that as Messiah he would spark off a revolt against the Roman occupying forces, Jesus gave strict instructions to the disciples not to break the astonishing news (v.21). Bringing in the kingdom of God was to involve other things, both for Christ and for Christians.

The Way For Christ Far from leading a triumphant popular uprising, Jesus went on to say that as Messiah he would be rejected and killed (v.22) The Old Testament prophets had certainly forecast this (read Isaiah 53.12 for instance); now Jesus confirmed their words. About a week later (v.28) during an extraordinary meeting with Moses and Elijah, the only topic of conversation mentioned is his death (v.31). Jesus was under no illusions about the cost involved in redeeming the world. But while his death was a tragedy, it was not an accident. It had all been foretold (look ahead to 22.37). Yet the cross was not to be the end of the story. Firstly, Jesus said that he would rise from the dead after three days (v.22); then, he spoke of returning to earth in triumphant glory (v.26); finally, he heard the Father's voice of loving assurance when he was transfigured on the mountain-top (v.35). Jesus knew that there was a crown beyond the cross. Make a careful note of the significance of this in Hebrews 12.2!

The Way For Christians The passage also tells us that Christians have a parallel (though not identical) experience. The Christian must "take up his cross" (v.23), that is to say, he must die to all his own self-centred desires, ambitions and aims. What is more, he must do it "daily". Christian living is not a matter of fits and starts, but rather of continuous discipline and dedication. Emphasising the point, Jesus said that the Christian must "lose his life", abandoning self-satisfaction as a philosophy. But such living brings its reward. Notice how this comes across in the passage. Firstly, Jesus said that the person who lost his life in this way would "save it" (v.24). Then, the appearance of Moses and Elijah would have been a great encouragement to Peter, James and John, and an assurance to them of a life of glory beyond the grave. Notice that when Peter referred to it later, it was immediately after a reference to his own death (2 Peter 1.13-18). To bear the cross is to prepare for the crown!

"We share in his sufferings in order that we may also share in his glory" (Romans 8.17 NIV)

28

Disappointing Disciples and Others

Luke 9.37-62

Today's rather longer reading gathers up five incidents which can help us to learn from the failings of the people they describe. Like the rest of the Bible, these verses were "written for our instruction" (Romans 15.4 AMP). The five incidents point out at least four flaws in the people concerned.

Unbelief (vv.37-45) When Jesus came down from the mountain he was immediately surrounded by a crowd (v.37). One man was in terrible distress because his son was demon-possessed and suffering from screaming fits and convulsions (v.39). He had asked the disciples to heal him, but they had not been able to do so (v.40). Even as they were speaking, the boy was thrown to the ground by the evil spirit (v.42). Jesus immediately rebuked the evil spirit, healed the boy and tenderly restored him to his father (v.42). But notice the rebuke in verse 41. Perhaps the crowd in general is included in this, but Matthew 17.19-20 seems to indicate those who were especially guilty! As we can see from vv.43-45, they were not even clear yet about how Jesus was to fulfil his mission. In spite of all they had seen Jesus do, and of the power they had been given (check this back at v.1) they were still weakened by unbelief. For the world at large, this was predictable because predicted (see John 12.37-38) — but it was a great tragedy for disciples of Christ. Are you living at the level of God's promises? How do you react, for intance, to 2 Corinthians 1.20 and 7.1?

Pride (vv.46-48) Coming so soon after what Jesus said at v.44, the words of v.46 are shocking. Were some of them jealous of Peter, James and John? Knowing what was in their minds, Jesus used a child as a visual aid (v.47). He taught them that to render lowly service in his name was to serve him, and that true humility had its own reward (v.48). Beware of pride on any part of your Christian life and service. In the light of Matthew 5.48 such a thing is both ignorant and sinful!

Intolerance (vv.49-56) There are two incidents here. In the first, the disciples reported that they had put a stop to a man casting out devils in Christ's name because he was not a member of their group. Were they jealous of his success? (Link v.49 with 4.40!) Perhaps they expected to be commended; instead, Jesus corrected them and told them "whoever is not against you is for you" (v.50 NIV). Joshua had made a similar mistake (see Numbers 11.24-30). Beware of negatively criticising those seeking to do God's work without toeing your particular party line. In the second incident, the disciples wanted God to incinerate the Samaritans who openly rejected Jesus! In reply, he said that that kind of spirit was wholly alien to Christians (v.55). His own purpose in coming into the world pointed the right way (v.56). Notice how the Bible says we are to deal with those who oppose the Christian message (2 Timothy 2.24-26).

Half-Heartedness (vv.57-62) In these verses, three unknown people flirt briefly with the idea of becoming Christians. The first sounded full of enthusiasm (v.57) but had failed to count the cost (v.58). The second wanted to wait until his father had died (v.59); but that might have been years away, and the kingdom of God made a more urgent claim. (v.60) The third made a seemingly innocent request (v.61), but Jesus detected a weakness, and insisted that a Christian must keep his eyes firmly fixed in one direction (v.62). Contrast these people with the Apostle Paul (see Philippians 3.12-14)— and think carefully where you stand!

"Caleb ... wholly followed the Lord" (Dueteronomy 1.36)

29
Ambassadors For Christ
Luke 10.1-24

These verses record the sending out by Jesus of a second wave of evangelistic commandoes. Manuscripts differ as to whether there were seventy or seventy-two (v.1), but much more important were the context and nature of their ministry. Three words will help us to capture some of the truth in this passage.

Responsibility Their mission was one involving great *danger;* they would be like lambs among wolves (v.3). It was to be made in great *dependence* – much the same as the twelve sent out earlier, they were to take neither "purse or bag or (spare?) sandals" (v.4 NIV). And it was to be a mission involving great *dedication;* they were not to waste time in idle chatter (compare v.4 with 2 Kings 4.29), in quibbling over ceremonial food regulations (v.7) or in endless social activities (v.7). Their mission was urgent and important. By divine appointment (v.1) they were involved in nothing less than "the kingdom of God" (v.9) and when they spoke they would do so in the Lord's name (see v.16). As with the previous group, they were authorised and empowered to heal and to preach (v.9) — but notice another responsibility (v.2). We need constantly to examine ourselves in all of these areas. As ambassadors for Christ (see 2 Corinthians 5.20) we are under a solemn obligation to fulfil our God-given mandate. We may not be what we call 'full-time', but we must be whole-hearted. In passing, notice that a great responsibility also rested on those who heard their preaching (vv.10-15). Sodom, Tyre and Sidon had all come under the judgment of God because of their sin; the fate of those who rejected the clear preaching of the gospel would be even worse. To realise that will surely make us more determined than ever to preach the gospel faithfully and plainly.

Revelation The fact that these messengers were appointed by the Lord can now be linked to words he spoke to his Father (vv.21-22) and to them on their return (vv.23-24). In the first two verses we are told that Christianity is not a matter of human research or reasoning, but of divine revelation. "These things" would refer to the general body of truth Jesus had taught the disciples; but the crucial truth centred around the related identities of God the Father and God the Son. Only Jesus could reveal this to men. This is a fundamental biblical truth; take time to read 1 Corinthians 2.9-14 and 2 Corinthians 4.3-6 very carefully, and notice how this all fits into the context of evangelism. In verses 23-24 we are told that the first disciples were given the added privilege of a physical revelation. Generations of Jews had longed for the Messiah; these men were actually seeing him. No wonder Jesus called them "blessed" (v.23). We too should rejoice at all that the Lord has been pleased to reveal to us in his Word.

Rejoicing When the disciples returned from their mission, they gave an excited report about the success of it all (v.17). In reply, Jesus said three things. Firstly, he said that he had seen Satan himself fall from heaven (v.18). He may have said this in order to put their triumphs in perspective, or to warn them against the danger of pride, which caused Satan's downfall (1 Timothy 3.6). Secondly, he reminded them that the authority and power they had was not self-generated; it had been given to them by him (v.19). Thirdly, he taught that a man's main cause for rejoicing should not be his Christian service, but his Christian status (v.20). When a person has reason to believe that his name is written in "the book of life" (Philippians 4.3) then he has reason not to boast (for it was none of his doing) but to rejoice.

"Come ... inherit the kingdom prepared for you" (Matthew 25.34)

30
A Day Of Questions
Luke 10.25-42

Today's reading includes what may be the best-known story in the Bible, the Parable of the Good Samaritan. It is also one of the most misused, and subject to interpretations that are sometimes fascinating but often false. We can keep to the real meaning of the story by taking careful note of the questions that surround it.

Question 1 The "lawyer" of v.25 would have been an expert in Old Testament religion, specialising in the law of Moses, contained in the first five books. His first question was deliberately asked "to test Jesus" (v.25 NIV). He wanted to know how this wandering Galilean preacher would answer an important question very much in people's minds at the time (compare 18.18).

Questions 2 And 3 In return, Jesus asked two parallel questions which pinned the man down to his specialist subject, "the law" (v.26). The man's reply showed a very clear grasp of the Old Testament, for in quoting from Deuteronomy 6.5 and Leviticus 19.18 he was crystallising the Ten Commandments, just as Jesus did at Mark 12.29-31. Now in theory he was right; the man who kept the law perfectly would "live" (v.28). But as no man had ever done so, gaining eternal life by keeping the law was a purely hypothetical notion. The law's real intention was quite different (see Romans 3.20 and Galatians 3.23-24). However, Jesus took the man up on his answer and said *"Do this* and you will live" (v.28 NIV). Realising that he was now trapped into admitting his own failure (and therefore the insincerity of his first question) the lawyer tried to justify himself by raising a point of interpretation.

Question 4 According to their traditional teaching, the

59

Jews were under no obligation to love those outside of their own race and religion. These people were not their "neighbours". If Jesus confirmed this line of thought, the man would be off the hook! — so the lawyer asked "And who is my neighbour?" (v.29). In reply, Jesus told a story. A man travelling on the notorious Jericho Road was beaten, robbed, and left for dead (v.30). Some time later a priest came along, took one look at him, and hurried on (v.31). Then a Levite (another religious official) came along and did likewise (v.32). Notice that these two not only left the dying man there, they "passed by on the other side" (vv.31-32). Presumably they thought he was dead, and did not want to become ceremonially unclean by touching a dead body (see Numbers 19.11). Then a Samaritan came along. Seeing the wounded man, he rushed to give him first-aid, took him to an inn, and agreed to pay for his entire convalescence! (vv.33-35) The people would have been stunned by this, as the Jews and the Samaritans were constantly at loggerheads (see John 4.9).

Question 5 The lawyer had asked a question about *identifying* a neighbour; Jesus now asked a question about *being* one (v.36). The answer was obvious (v.37) and the implication inescapable (v.37). However else this story is used, its real purpose is to show that *everyone* is our "neighbour", and that we are to give whatever help we can to those we find in need, regardless of race, rank, colour, creed, or anything else. To think this through is to realise that here is the very heart of practical Christianity.

In closing this section, Luke inserts an incident at Bethany (vv.38-42). The narrative speaks for itself. Perhaps Luke put it in alongside the story of the Good Samaritan to balance the lawyer's pre-occupation with the "second commandment". Only the Christian prepared to sit at the feet of Jesus will be able to stand in the face of the world! Worship comes before service, and the King before the King's business (see Matthew 4.10).

"O worship the Lord in the beauty of holiness" (Psalm 96.9)

31
How To Pray
Luke 11.1-13

Every Christian should identify with the disciples when they asked Jesus to meet one of man's greatest spiritual needs — "Lord, teach us to pray" (v.1); and should be profoundly grateful that the New Testament preserves for all time the answer he gave. His reply covers thirteen verses in Luke's account, and for study purposes can usefully be divided into three parts.

The Pattern He Gave (vv.2-4) These words, together with the version at Matthew 6.9-13, are probably the best-known in the whole Bible. We usually call them "The Lord's Prayer", though we can be sure there was at least one part of it that Jesus never used at all (link the beginning of v.4 with Hebrews 4.15 for the reason). The opening words of verse 2 show that Jesus meant us to use this prayer as it is (compare Matthew 6.9). The Jews were quite familiar with set, formal prayers, and Rabbis often taught them to their followers (notice the end of v.1 where John is said to have done the same thing). But it is also a model for *all* prayer — in three ways. *Firstly*, because of what it says about God. It puts God first; (notice the first three petitions, in verse 2). Prayer is not meant to be a selfish shopping-list. Our first concern should be for God's glory (see Deuteronomy 26.2 and Matthew 6.33). *Secondly*, because of what it says about man; as verse 3 shows, man is utterly dependent on God's goodness and provision, even for his physical survival (so much for the devil's lie at Genesis 3.5!). *Thirdly*, because of what it says about sin; the three final petitions are all about the same subject, which obviously infers that holiness of life should be the Christian's constant concern (check 1 Thessalonians 4.3 where its importance is put in the simplest possible terms).

The Parable He Told (vv.5-10) The story is not without humour! In a tiny Jewish home, there would normally be just one room, and the family would sleep on the floor, huddled together for warmth in a raised part farthest from the door. The split-level design would allow for the domestic animals to sleep in the same room, but on the lower level, nearest the door. For the man of the house to open the door to a midnight caller would almost certainly mean disturbing the sleeping children (v.7) — to say nothing of causing chaos among the chickens! But in the story the visitor refused to give in, so the man had to get up! There are probably two lessons here. One is the need to persist in prayer; "importunity" in v.8 literally means "shamelessness"! — the Amplified Bible has "shameless persistence and insistence". Jesus was to devote a whole parable to this later on (see Luke 18.1-8, and especially v.1 which gives the reason for that parable). But the primary lesson of the parable told here was underlined in another way.

The Principle He Established (vv.11-13) The key phrase here is *"how much more* shall your heavenly Father" (v.13). Notice now how the whole passage slots together. The questions in vv.11-12 are about *fathers,* who for all their human sinfulness, give good things to their children (v.13); the householder in the parable is a *father,* but also a friend (see v.5), who, even if reluctantly, will not leave his friend in need; and at the beginning of The Lord's Prayer, Christians are encouraged to pray to "Our *Father"* (v.2)! God is not a miser, reluctant to give; on the contrary, he longs to pour out blessing on his children, for whom there is no greater gift than the Holy Spirit (see v.13 and compare with Psalm 84.11). The whole of this record could be summed up in this way—the *pattern* tells us that we should pray inclusively; the *parable* tells us that we should pray persistently; the *principle* tells us that we should pray expectantly!

"If any of you lacks…he should ask God, who gives generously to all" (James 1.5 NIV)

32

Jesus — Deity Or Devil?
Luke 11.14-36

Throughout his public ministry, Jesus was the centre of controversy (see John 7.43 for instance); a fact which carries with it the incidental lesson that even at our best we will not always meet with approval. Here, as elsewhere, his very nature was being questioned. It will help us in our study if we divide this somewhat longer passage into five sections.

Accusation (vv.14-16) When Jesus restored a man's speech by casting out a spirit of dumbness, "the crowd was amazed" (v.14 NIV). But some people flatly accused him of using satanic power ("Beelzebub", in v.15, was probably a corruption of the name of a heathen Philistine god—see 2 Kings 1.2—and was commonly used as a Jewish synonym for the devil). However, not everybody agreed with such an appalling assessment; instead, they asked Jesus to give them some kind of supernatural indication that the source of his power lay elsewhere (v.16).

Argument (vv.17-20) Jesus began his reply with cool and unanswerable logic. Surely evil set against evil could only mean self-destruction? (v.17) Was satan out to defeat himself? (v.18) And what about other Jews who had cast out devils—were they also in league with the devil? (v.19) There is a fine and important lesson in all of this cut and thrust; whilst we are never to be argumentative (see 2 Timothy 2.23-25) we must not be afraid of using strong, forceful argument (compare Paul's example at Acts 19.8). Christian witness involves hard, careful thinking, not just throwing clumps of texts at people!

Attestation (vv.20-22) So far the kind of argument Jesus was using inferred that he was using Divine power; now he said so plainly (v.20). The devil is "strong" (v.21) but God is "stronger" (v.22) and when he attacks, satan's defenses are powerless. This was exactly what Jesus had been doing—what more attestation could they need? It is interesting to link together John 14.11 and John 3.3!

Application (vv.23-36; 29-36) But notice that this is no idle theorising; it has many practical applications. In the first place, there can be no neutrality on the question of who Jesus is (v.23). Nobody can sit on the fence here; a man must make up his mind (compare 1 Kings 18.21). Then, being a Christian does not just mean agreeing to an occasional spring-clean, it means the discipline of a permanent moral revolution (vv.24-26). Only God can bring about the desire for that change, and the change itself. Only the Holy Spirit can banish evil spirits. Thirdly, those who reject the clear evidence Christ gave will be condemned (vv.29-32). As we saw, some Jews had asked Jesus for "a sign" (v.16) — but the only one he would give them was one they did not want, his own resurrection! (see Matthew 12.40 for the link with Jonah). The heathen Ninevites had repented when Jonah preached to them (Jonah 3.5), and Jesus was greater than Jonah (v.32); the Queen of Sheba had been convinced by the wisdom of Solomon (1 Kings 10.4-9), and Jesus was greater than Solomon (v.31). The Jews were without excuse. Finally, just as a man must be clear-eyed to walk safely (v.34) so he must be clear-minded on spiritual issues if his life is to be "wholly bright with light" (v.36 AMP.).

Adoration (vv.27-28) Yet in the midst of all the disbelief, doubt and downright opposition, at least one voice—a woman's — was raised in recognition and adoration (v.27). Jesus replied to this inspired exclamation with a reminder that knowledge demands obedience (v.28). The New Testament knows no other kind of Christianity—see Revelation 22.14. Are you living up to the light you have?

"Give unto the Lord the glory due unto his name" (1 Chronicles 16.29)

33
Beware The Woes Of Jesus!
Luke 11.37-54

It all began with a dinner-party (v.37) but before he left the house in which the meal was held Jesus had revealed the terrible spiritual condition of many of the guests. Six times in this passage he uses the exclamation "Woe!" Although not a word of final judgement, it does contain a serious warning. Be prepared to expose your own life to the light of God's word as we examine what Jesus found in these people.

Law Instead of Love (vv.38-42) The discussion was sparked off when Jesus failed to wash his hands before eating (v.38). (The hand-washing referred to was a fantastic ceremonial rigmarole, and had nothing to do with hygiene.) In reply to his host's amazement, Jesus pronounced his first "Woe!" (v.42) — on those who paid meticulous attention to ceremonial and traditional details of the law (see vv.39 and 42) but were inwardly "full of greed and robbery and extortion and malice and wickedness" (v.39 AMP). They were more concerned with man-made laws than with "the love of God" (v.42).

Pomp Instead Of Piety (v.43) For many of the Pharisees, church-going was no more than an opportunity to display themselves. The "uppermost seats in the synagogues" were in full public view and were reserved for distinguished guests. The Pharisees made sure that they were never empty! But no man can exalt himself and God at the same time. Isaiah 42.8 and John 3.30 are worth reading in this connection!

Hindrance Instead Of Help (v.44) Jewish graves were usually well marked with some kind of whitewash so that people would know exactly where they were, as any contact with a grave would cause the person concerned to become ceremonially defiled. Jesus now accused some of the Pharisees of being like "unmarked graves" (NIV). As religious leaders, they should have been a help to others, whereas by their actions and attitudes they were often a positive hindrance to those who came into contact with them. Take another look back at v.23. Is your life, taken as a whole, likely to draw people to Christ or drive them from him?

Preaching Instead Of Practising (vv.45-46) The "lawyers" were Old Testament students, closely linked to the Pharisees. One of them now protested that Jesus was tarring all of them with the same brush (v.45). In reply, Jesus singled them out for special criticism! For example, they insisted on people keeping all the fantastic details of their man-made religious laws, while they themselves found ways of avoiding them (v.46). Notice Paul's words about this at Romans 2.17-23. The Christian should always practise what he preaches, and not just because actions speak louder than words.

Ritual Instead Of Repentance (v.47-51) By Hebrew chronology, Abel (Genesis 4.8) and Zechariah (2 Chronicles 24.20-21) were the first and last Old Testament martyrs. By elaborate attention to the tombs of martyred prophets (v.47) the lawyers tried to exempt themselves from guilt (see Matthew 23.30). But their ritualistic sorrow was sheer hypocrisy — after all, they were planning to kill the greatest Prophet of all! — see vv.53-54. No wonder Jesus said what he did at verse 50.

Ignorance Instead Of Insight (v.52) Though they were Bible students, they had so perverted and complicated the scriptures that they had missed their saving message, and even confused people on the brink of grasping it. What a solemn challenge to us to submit to the plain teaching of scripture, and to be crystal clear when sharing it with others!

"Search me, O God, and know my heart" (Psalm 139.23)

34
Warnings And
Encouragements (1)
Luke 12.1-21

Luke now brings together various sayings of Jesus which
were possibly not spoken at the same time, nor even
necessarily in the order given here. The connecting link
is that when put together they form a series of warnings
and encouragements. Matthew 24.35 tells us why every
one of them is relevant to us today. We shall cover the
whole passage (ending at Luke 13.9) in the course of the
next three studies.

Be Warned! — Truth Will Out (vv.1-3) The besetting sin
of the Pharisees was hypocrisy — glance through
Matthew 23.13-29 and make a careful note of how many
times Jesus denounced them for this. But while hypocrisy (pretending to be what we are not) may deceive
others, it can never deceive God — as Hebrews 4.13
makes perfectly clear — and on the day of judgment the
whole truth will be fully and finally revealed. Notice
Paul's solemn words in Romans 2.16 — and with those
words in mind turn to Peter's instructions in 1 Peter 1.17.

Be Encouraged! — God Counts Sparrows (vv.4-9; 11-12)
Having pointed out that God's judgment is so certain,
and so infallible, Jesus went on to emphasise another
point. Even the fear of martyrdom should give way before the fear of God — because even the most vicious
tyrants' power is limited. There comes a point at which
there is "no more that they can do" (v.4). On the other
hand, God has power not only to put an end to physical
life but also to condemn a man to eternal punishment in
hell (v.5). We should be more afraid of losing God's
favour than of losing our lives! Yet this "fear" of God is
not terror, because God is a God of amazing love and
infinite care, as Jesus now illustrated by his reference to
the sparrows (vv.6-7). Sparrows normally sold at two for a

farthing (Matthew 10.29) but there seemed to be a discount for quantity, which meant that if you bought four, you got an extra one free! (v.6) Yet God's providential care extends even to creatures of such little value—"not one of them is forgotten or uncared for in the presence of God" (v.6 AMP). As for human beings, God is intimately concerned about the minutest detail of our lives (v.7). That being so, we should never be ashamed of him (vv.8-9), and be assured that if we find ourselves in a situation in which we are being persecuted for righteousness' sake, we can rely on the guidance and enabling of the Holy Spirit (vv.11-12). Notice carefully, however, that this is a promise for the dock, and not for the pulpit!

Be Warned!—There Is An Unforgivable Sin (v.10) The Holy Spirit's great ministry is to bear witness to the truth about Jesus Christ (see John 16.13-14). To blaspheme against the Holy Spirit is to reject his witness altogether. When a person continues to do that there is no hope for him, because he is rejecting God's only way of salvation. This verse has caused many people great distress because they have misunderstood its meaning; but the person who is anxious that he may have committed the unforgivable sin has almost certainly not done so, or he would have no sorrow or concern about displeasing God or rejecting the clear witness that he gives about his Son.

Be Warned!—Greed Is Insane (vv.13-21) At this point a man seems to have interrupted Jesus, asking him to arbitrate in a family squabble over inheritance (v.13). Jesus firmly refused to get involved (v.14) but took the opportunity of pointing out that possessions do not make a man rich (make a careful note of v.15). He drove his point home with a simple but telling parable (vv.16-20). Greed is insane, because we will lose all our material possessions the moment we die—and that may be "this night" (v.20)! Proverbs 11.4 will then put all our riches in context.

"Set your minds on things above, not on earthly things" (Colossians 3.2 NIV)

35
Warnings And Encouragements (2)
Luke 12.22-48

Today's reading takes in the second of three sections in this part of Luke's Gospel in which he records various sayings of Jesus which, when taken together, form a series of warnings and encouragements.

Be Encouraged! — Your Father Is A King (vv.22-34) In warning people about greed, Jesus had told a parable about a wealthy and successful farmer (vv.16-21). But wealth can be a stumbling-block not only to the rich but to the poor. One is tempted to gloat and the other to fret; one sins because of the lot he has, and the other over the little he has. Yet Jesus taught that it was wrong to be anxious, even about necessities. The whole lesson of these verses could be summed up in one phrase—"do not *worry*" (v.22 NIV). Verse 25 illustrates the futility of worry very well. The word "cubit" probably refers to length of time rather than height (a cubit was about 21 inches, and to grow that much taller could hardly be called "a very little thing"! (v.26 NIV). The sense seems to be that nobody can extend his life by worrying about it—as a matter of fact, the reverse is almost certainly the case! Jesus backed up his arguments with a number of simple illustrations from nature. The birds of the air (v.24) and the flowers and grass in the fields (vv.27-28) are vivid examples of God's amazing and adequate provision. The Bible does not encourage Christians to be lazy or careless, or to rely on others for their maintenance — notice carefully what Paul says in 2 Thessalonians 3.7-12 — but we must marry our personal responsibility to God's permanent reliability, and remember that as far as the necessities of life are concerned, our Father knows what we need (v.30). What is more, he has promised to give us not only these earthly things, but the Kingdom of God itself (v.32). It is therefore quite wrong for us to be "seized with alarm and struck with fear" (v.32 AMP). On the contrary, our only concern should be that we seek this kingdom by living godly, obedient lives. God promises that if we make that our concern he will make all the other things his concern, which is a cast-iron guarantee that we shall receive all that we need (v.31).

Be Encouraged! — Jesus Is Coming (vv.35-40) The Christian has yet another motive for sitting loose to material possessions—Jesus is coming back and may do so at any time (v.40). That being so, we should be constantly on the alert (vv.35-36). John sums up what this will mean in terms of our daily lives (1 John 3.2-3). When that great event occurs, the faithful and obedient servants will receive a reward that Jesus described in the most astonishing terms (v.37)—though we are not given any detailed explanation of what this will mean. No wonder Jesus said that at that day "it will be good for those servants" (v.37 NIV)!

Be Warned! — Servants Are Accountable (vv.41-48) After hearing this parable, Peter appeared to ask whether it referred to all Christians, or just to the inner circle of apostles (v.41). To answer his question, Jesus told another parable, the gist of which could be summed up like this: while all servants are responsible, those with special privileges have special responsibilities. In the parable, the "faithful and wise manager" (v.42 NIV) was promoted as a reward for his services. But if a man in the same position of authority had misused his office (v.45) he would be severely punished (v.46). Knowledge, responsibility and accountability go together and we must give serious weight to everything the Bible has to say about God's perfect justice both in granting rewards and in administering punishment (vv.47-48). Notice how this is put in James 3.1 and James 4.17.

"Those who have been given a trust must prove faithful" (1 Corinthians 4.2 NIV)

36
Warnings And Encouragements (3)
Luke 12.49-13.9

Today's reading completes the section beginning at Luke 12.1 in which Jesus issues a number of warnings and at the same time gives words of encouragement to his followers. These final verses cover five main truths, all of them in the nature of warnings.

Be Warned!—Truth Divides (vv.49-53) These verses are a sobering reminder that genuine Christianity has radical consequences. When Jesus spoke of his coming "baptism", and added "and how distressed I am until it is completed" (v.50 NIV) he was referring to his crucifixion (compare Mark 10.33-34) which would overwhelm him with grief (see Matthew 26.38 and Luke 22.44). While that great sacrifice would save multitudes of people, it would also lead to "fire" (v.49) and "division" (v.51). This is a difficult passage to analyse in a clear yet concise way but there does seem to be one obvious way in which "fire" and "division" can be linked together. As Christians began to make a moral and spiritual impact on society, men would become enflamed with opposition to the gospel, and there would even be times when persecution for the gospel's sake would divide members of the same family from each other (vv.52-53). This kind of opposition may be hard to bear and difficult to understand, but we must remember that in his perfect wisdom God allows persecution in order that his church might be purified (see 1 Peter 1.6-7).

Be Warned! — History Is Speaking (vv.54-56). Some of the Jews seemed to be good amateur weather-forecasters! (link v.54 with Matthew 16.2-3). But Jesus told them that whatever their skill at interpreting the clouds and the wind, they were hopelessly ignorant of the things that really mattered (v.56). The Christian should live with his newspaper in one hand and his Bible in the other—and learn to interpret the first in the light of the second!

Be Warned! — The Judge Is Waiting (vv.57-59) Jesus next pointed out that some people were so taken up with trivialities, they had lost all sense of proportion and judgment (v.57). They had even become careless about their own standing in God's sight. Jesus compared them to a man and his accuser on their way to court (v.58). As the man concerned is clearly in the wrong — hence the likely sentence (vv.58-59)—the sensible attitude to adopt to the accuser is to "be reconciled to him on the way" (vv.58 NIV). In the same way, the certainty of condemnation should make a man look to God for mercy before he has to face his inevitable justice (link Psalm 2.12 with Acts 3.19).

Be Warned!—Repentance Is Essential (Chapter 13.1-5) This follows on perfectly. When someone told Jesus of the massacre of certain Jews on Pilate's instructions, he added another headline incident — the collapse of a building in Jerusalem (v.4) — and then issued a stern warning. Those who had died were no worse than other people (vv.2 and 4); but their sudden deaths should be a reminder to everyone of the necessity and urgency of repentance (vv.3 and 5).

Be Warned!—There Comes A Last Chance (vv.6-9) This "warning section comes to an end with a tiny but telling parable. The fig tree should have produced fruit, because it was planted in the fertile soil of a vineyard (v.6). Yet in three years it produced nothing and instructions were given to cut it down (v.7). The husbandman was able to secure just one year's stay of execution (v.8) but after that, judgment would be carried out (v.9). The Jews should have recognised the primary reference as being to their own nation (see Jeremiah 24.1-3 and Hosea 9.10) but the issue is not only national but personal. For some men, at a given moment of time, there may be another chance; for all men, there comes a last chance.

"Have mercy upon me, O Lord" (Psalm 31.9)

37
Keys Of The Kingdom (1)
Luke 13.10-21

When John the Baptist was preparing the way for the coming of Jesus, he told his hearers "the kingdom of heaven is at hand" (Matthew 3.2), while Jesus himself could not have been clearer about the significance of his ministry when he announced that "the kingdom of God is come unto you" (Matthew 12.28). Many of the things Jesus said and did can be most easily understood when we read them in the context of the kingdom of God, and we will do this for our two remaining studies in Luke 13.

The Overall Spirit Of The Kingdom While living in his home town of Nazareth Jesus had been a regular worshipper at the local synagogue (see Luke 4.16) and he often taught in synagogues in the course of his itinerant ministry (see Mark 1.39). At this point in his life the opposition to him was mounting, with the result that this is the last recorded visit he paid to a synagogue. One Sabbath day he saw a crippled woman in the congregation. Full of compassion for her, he called her over and immediately cured her of a disease that had gripped her for 18 years (v.13). The ruler of the synagogue (the official responsible for all that went on there) complained to the people, suggesting that if there were others who needed healing, they should come on some other day of the week! (v.14) The reason for his outburst was that Jewish leaders had added to God's law about the Sabbath a mass of complicated regulations, and under these man-made laws Jesus could be accused of working, and therefore breaking the fourth Commandment (see Exodus 20.9-11). In reply, Jesus accused the ruler of blatant hypocrisy (v.15). Their Sabbath laws allowed the Jews to have mercy on thirsty animals; surely it was within the spirit of God's law for Jesus to have mercy on this suffering woman? (vv.15-16) The kingdom of God is concerned with more important things than man-made religious paraphernalia (see Romans 14.17 and Colossians 2.20); and with nothing more important than the overthrow of the devil (link v.16 with Hebrews 2.14-15).

The Ultimate Success Of The Kingdom Jesus then told two tiny "kingdom of God" parables, both taken from ordinary, everyday life. A "grain of mustard seed" (v.19) is very small (see what is said about it in Mark 4.31) but in favourable Middle East conditions it grows rapidly into a plant big enough to be called a tree (v.19). Jesus was making the point that whatever opposition it faced, the kingdom of God was invincible, and people from all nations would eventually become a part of it (look ahead to v.29). Old Testament scholars would perhaps have remembered prophecies like Ezekiel 17.22-24 which used birds as a symbol for the nations of the world — and to those words we can add the marvellous promise of Isaiah 53.10-11. Whatever men might try to do to stop it, God has guaranteed the triumph of his gospel kingdom!

The Inner Strength Of The Kingdom In the second parable, Jesus said that the kingdom of God was like "yeast" (v.21 NIV). The "three measures of meal" would be about 40 litres—a large amount—but the apparently insignificant yeast would quietly penetrate it all (v.21). The picture is clear. Christians are meant to penetrate society for Christ, changing its moral texture by the powerful influence of God-energised lives. In the worlds of politics, education, sport, music, medicine, art and other areas of social life we should be quietly and humbly at work. The Christian minority made a great impact in the early days of the church (see Acts 17.6) and Christians have often pioneered enormous social changes down the years. We dare not opt out of our responsibility in this whole area.

"God . . . calls you into his kingdom and glory" (1 Thessalonians 2.12 NIV)

38
Keys Of The Kingdom (2)
Luke 13.22-35

As Luke continues to record a number of scattered incidents, he reminds us that they all took place as Jesus was gradually making his way towards Jerusalem (v.22). Today's reading takes in three incidents that probably occurred at quite different times.

The Priority Jesus Urged The teaching in this section (vv.22-30) was given in answer to a very important question (v.23). The Jews were constantly discussing this very point — although many of them believed that the kingdom of God was theirs by right of inheritance (see John 8.31-33, for instance). In his reply Jesus ignored the statistical point *(how many* would be saved) and concentrated on the spiritual *(who* would be saved). Many who imagine that they will be saved because of some vague association with Jesus (v.26) will in fact be lost (v.27). Elsewhere, we are told of others with even higher hopes but who will also be excluded from heaven (see Matthew 7.21-23). No wonder Paul says what he does at 2 Corinthians 13.5! Jesus made it clear that the door of the kingdom of God was "narrow" (v.24 NIV) and a man must "strive to enter in" (v.24). This does not mean that a man is saved by self-effort—Jesus said exactly the opposite at the end of verse 24 — but that salvation is a matter of extreme urgency. The day will come when the door would be closed, and it will be too late (v.25). It will then be especially galling for proud but unconverted Jews to see Gentiles from all over the world inside the kingdom of God (v.29) and they themselves shut out. The challenge of these verses can be put in the form of two questions: Are you in? Are you trying to bring others in?

The Purpose Jesus Maintained Luke next records

some of the Pharisees warning Jesus of an assassination attempt by Herod (v.31). Herod had already been disturbed by reports of Jesus' ministry. At one stage he even thought that Jesus must be a re-incarnation of John the Baptist, whom he had put to death (the story is told in Mark 6.14-29 — link this with Luke 9.7-9). The Pharisees' warning may therefore have been a false but deliberate "leak" to frighten Jesus out of Herod's territory of Galilee. Be that as it may, Jesus replied that nothing could prevent his life from running its God-appointed course, which would come to a climax with his death at Jerusalem (v.33). A recurring spirit of "I must" ran through the life of Jesus (see, for instance Luke 2.49 and John 9.4) and it was this sense of divine purpose that garrisoned his spirit against all opposition. Every Christian can go through life with the same certainty — based on truths like those expressed in Psalm 139, and especially vv.5-10.

The Plea Jesus Made Matthew places the words of vv.34-35 some time later, when Jesus was already at Jerusalem (Matthew 23.37-39). Luke probably inserted them here because of the mention of Jerusalem in verse 33. The city had a shocking record of violence against God's special messengers (see 2 Chronicles 24.21; 36.15-17 for instance). Yet those messengers had been tokens of God's mercy, and even now Jesus would gladly have welcomed the people of the city into his protective care (v.34). But by and large they were "not willing" (v.34 NIV). The result would be appalling (v.35) — words fulfilled literally when Jerusalem was destroyed in AD 70 and figuratively in that the man who rejects Christ is left with nothing (see John 6.53). Like the rest of the world, Jerusalem would have to recognise Jesus at his Second Coming (v.35) but by then it would be too late (compare Matthew 24.30). It is always costly to reject God's mercy.

"Today, if you hear his voice, do not harden your hearts" (Hebrews 3.7-8 NIV)

39
Words Of Wisdom
Luke 14.1-24

Even his enemies were often struck by the sheer moral power of Christ's teaching (compare Luke 4.22 with Matthew 13.54). What made his words even more striking was the fact that they were not all carefully prepared speeches or sermons. The setting for today's reading, for instance, is a meal in the house of a prominent Pharisee (v.1). But in the course of it Jesus had words for everyone who was present—and for all of us, who were not!

A Word For The Critics As we saw earlier, Jesus constantly infuriated the Pharisees by healing people on the Sabbath day (glance back to 6.6-11 and 13.10-17). Faced with yet another man in dire need—the word "dropsy" (v.2) means that the man's body was hideously swollen with excess fluid—Jesus asked the watching Pharisees a question (v.3). Getting no answer, he healed the man (v.4) and immediately asked another unanswerable question (vv.5-6). We may not always be able to please ecclesiastical fusspots, but we can rest assured that Spirit-filled living is never in conflict with God's law! (See Galatians 5.22-23)

A Word For The Guests As the meal was about to be served, Jesus noticed some of the guests worming their way into the most important places (v.7). This prompted him to tell a simple but pointed parable (vv.8-10). The maxim in verse 11 appears again in Matthew 23.12 and Luke 18.14, and the same truth is stated many times in the Old Testament (Proverbs 29.23 for instance). Pride makes a man small, however great he may seem to be; humility makes a man great, however small he may seem to be. The lesson is easy to learn, but difficult to live. James 4.10 should help!

A Word For The Host The meal seems to have been something of a closed shop, part of an endless round of invitations involving the same people. Jesus had a comment on this, too. (vv.12-14) The words in verse 12 do not mean that a man should refuse hospitality to an inner circle of family and friends, but rather that his kindness should break through that circle and benefit those with no means of repaying him. That kind of giving is a real test of a man's generosity—and it will be rewarded with God's blessing (v.14). The Bible makes specific promises to those who are generous to the poor — see Proverbs 19.17 and Matthew 19.21.

A Word For The Lost Many Jews believed that the Messiah's coming would be marked by a gigantic feast, and the words Jesus used moved one man to burst out with joyful anticipation of the event (v.15) — no doubt confident that as a Jew his own place was reserved! In reply, Jesus told what we might call "the parable of the excuses". Invitations to banquets were issued in two stages (compare vv.16-17 with Esther 5.8 and 6.14). In the parable, the invited guests began to cry off when the second invitation came. But they gave excuses rather than reasons. Would a man buy a field before he had seen it? (v.18) Could the oxen not be tested a day or so later? (v.19) Could the newly-wed not bring his wife? (v.20) Grieved at their refusal, the host sent his servant first into the city and then into the countryside, freely inviting the most unlikely people until his house was filled with guests (vv.21-23). The lesson was this: throughout the Old Testament God's prophets had been calling the people of Israel. Now, Jesus was bringing the second, urgent invitation (notice Hebrews 1.1-2). Yet the privileged Jews were rejecting it (compare John 5.39-40). As a result, many Gentiles (not directly included in the first invitation) would gladly accept the call to the feast and enter the kingdom of God (see how Paul expounds this in Romans 9).

"Go into all the world and preach the good news ..." (Mark 16.15 NIV)

40
Discipleship
Luke 14.25-35

Although the incidents in this part of Luke's narrative are sometimes unconnected and out of exact chronological order, they are all in the general context of Jesus making his way to Jerusalem (glance back to 9.51). This may explain the "great multitudes" who now flocked after him (v.25). Many must have thought that he was about to take the city by storm, throw out the Roman occupying forces, and set up an earthly kingdom. But nothing could have been further from the truth — see John 18.36! Jesus was on his way to be crucified, not crowned, and Christianity was to be no easy ride in the wake of a revolutionary folk hero. To drive this lesson home, Jesus suddenly stopped his enthusiastic followers in their tracks (notice the word "turned" in v.25) and solemnly laid down the terms of Christian discipleship. He said that there were conditions to be met, without which a man could not be his disciple (vv.26, 27 and 33). His three-fold use of the phrase "cannot be my disciple" point us to the specific conditions he mentioned.

The Prior Claim The words of verse 26 do not mean that we must literally hate the members of our own family. Apart from being an absurd religious requirement, this would flatly contradict one the the Ten Commandments (see Exodus 20.12) — and Jesus said that he had come not to destroy the law but to fulfil it (Matthew 5.17). In the sense in which it is used here, the word "hate" means to love less. There is a good example of this in the Old Testament (see Genesis 29.31-33). To be a true disciple of Jesus means that whenever there is a conflict of claims, his takes priority. This may produce difficulties (notice the three verses that come before Matthew's version of this teaching at Matthew 10.34-36) but there is no obedient alternative. Acts 5.29 puts the issue precisely!

The Painful Cross Verse 27 is simple but searching —
compare it with 9.23, and notice the word "daily" there.
Jesus was not, of course, suggesting that only Christians
put to death on a cross would rank as genuine disciples
— yet the picture he used was a vivid one. A man
carrying his cross to the place of execution had no
further plans of his own; he would have forfeited control of his life. In the same way, the true disciple is
marked by spiritual self-crucifixion — which can sometimes be agonisingly painful. To die to our own com-
forts, ambitions and plans is of the very essence of true
Christianity. Paul puts it perfectly in Galatians 2.20.

The Premeditated Cost Jesus next told two brief parables (vv.28-32). He applied their message by saying that
a disciple must "give up everything he has" (v.33 NIV).
The precise linking of this phrase to the parables is not
immediately obvious, but the gist of the teaching is
clear: no man can afford to think lightly about being a
Christian. A disciple must be prepared to pay any price
in order to please his Lord and Saviour, and at the same
time abandon all trust in his own resources and ability.
(Read Mark 8.34-38 for another expression of the same
line of teaching.) Luke now inserts Jesus's parable about
salt (compare vv.34-35 with Matthew 5.13 and Mark
9.50). Salt was used as a preservative, as flavouring, and
as a fertilizer. The inferior salt used in those days sometimes lost its saltiness by exposure to the elements, and
when it did so it was virtually useless. In the same way,
the Christian disciple whose character becomes diluted
with worldliness completely loses his effectiveness.
Christians should penetrate the world without ever becoming part of it.

"The disciple is not above his master" *(Matthew 10.24)*

41

Lost And Found (1)
Luke 15.1-10

This chapter of Luke's Gospel is taken up by three parables with the same theme. In today's study we shall look at the first two of these well-known stories. In trying to understand the meaning of these parables it is important to notice the circumstances in which Jesus originally told them. The situation was that "tax collectors and 'sinners' were all gathering around to hear him" (v.1 NIV). Tax collectors were despised by the Jews not only because they were employed by the Romans but because many of them swindled their own people by over-charging (Luke 19.8 hints at this sort of thing). The "sinners" were people who had no interest in the finer points of religious law, which the Pharisees considered all-important. To them, these people were just an ignorant and godless rabble (see John 7.45-49). That is why we read of their reaction in verse 2. How could Jesus possibly be a man of God if he associated so freely with the country's riff-raff? Little did they realise it, but their miserable muttering was to trigger off some of the most wonderful teaching in the New Testament!

The Lost Sheep The first parable (vv.3-6) asked a question to which there could only be one answer. It would be obvious to everybody that the shepherd's active concern would be for the one sheep astray in dangerous "open country" (v.4 NIV) and he would do everything he could to recover it. When he found it, he would gladly carry it home (v.5). In that part of the world, flocks tended to be quite small, so that even one sheep would be very valuable. This meant that when the lost animal was safely back in the flock it was cause for great celebration (v.6). Jesus then drew out the lesson of the parable (v.7). There are several quite reasonable interpretations of the phrase "ninety-nine righteous persons who do not need to repent" (v.7 NIV). It may well be that Jesus was making an ironical reference to the self-righteous Pharisee (see 18.11 for an example of this). Be that as it may, the central thing Jesus wanted to get across was that God was lovingly concerned for lost sinners, and rejoiced when they turned from their sin.

The Lost Silver The second parable (vv.8-9) was equally simple. The "ten pieces of silver" (v.8) may have formed a married woman's headdress or necklace (the equivalent of today's wedding ring) or they may have been coins, one of which was the equivalent of a day's wage for a working man. The original word, *drachma,* is still in use in Greece today. In either case sentimentally or commercially, the piece of silver was valuable and important to the owner, and when she discovered that it was missing, she began a thorough search of the house. (v.8) Having told the story, Jesus added the same postscript as he did to the first one: one sinner turning from his sin was a cause for great rejoicing in heaven (v.10). Taken together, then, these two parables teach two great truths, both of which would have staggered the supercilious Pharisees. The first was that God is lovingly concerned to reach out to those who have rejected him and gone their own, sinful way (compare Ezekiel 33.11 and Luke 19.10); the second is that God welcomes with open arms the worst of sinners who honestly turn to him for forgiveness (see 2 Peter 3.9). To the Christian there are the incidental but important lessons that we should show genuine love for even the unloveliest of people, and unjudgingly welcome all Christians as brothers and sisters in Christ.

"God our Saviour ... wants all men to be saved and to come to a knowledge of the truth" (1 Timothy 2.3-4 NIV)

42
Lost And Found (2)
Luke 15.11-32

We come now to one of the most familiar stories in the whole Bible, usually called The Parable of the Prodigal Son. There are many ways in which it can be approached and analysed: in this study we shall use five words to hold together the main thread of the story.

Rebellion According to Jewish law, the younger of two sons would be entitled to one-third of his father's estate (see Deuteronomy 21.17). The division of the property and goods was usually made after the father's death, but in this case the self-willed son demanded his rights in advance (v.12). Soon afterwards, he left for some far-off country, where he "squandered his wealth in wild living" (v.13 NIV).

Ruin We are not told how long this wild extravagance went on, but eventually he ran out of money (v.14). Even worse, the country in which he was living was hit by a terrible famine (v.14). With an empty purse and an empty stomach, he looked for work, but the only job available was looking after pigs (v.15). Nothing could have been more disgusting for a Jew, to whom the pig was "unclean" by law (see Leviticus 11.7 and Deuteronomy 14.8). Things got so bad that he would gladly have eaten "the pods (of the carob tree) that the pigs were eating" (v.16 NIV). There is a high cost in low living—Psalm 34.21 is just one of the many places where the Bible makes this solemnly clear.

Reflection When he was at rock bottom, the young man finally "came to his senses" (v.17 NIV). Even his father's servants were better off than he was (v.17). He would go back home, confess his stupidity and sin, and ask to be employed as a servant (vv.18-19).

Repentance Notice carefully that he immediately put his thoughts and words into action — "he arose, and came to his father" (v.20). Repentance means more than recognising sin, or even regretting it; it means forsaking sin and turning to God. Look up Matthew 3.7-8 and notice how John the Baptist dealt with those who wanted acceptance without repentance!

Reception Verses 20-24 are the real heart of the story, showing the father's loving forgiveness as immediate (v.20) compassionate (v.20) and extravagantly generous (vv.22-24). Many fanciful interpretations have been given to other details of the story, but we must remember that a parable was normally told to illustrate one main point. A parable is a window, not an exhibition of coloured glass! As with the stories of the lost sheep and the lost silver, Jesus wanted to illustrate the overwhelming love of God. The Old Testament had already taught this (see Deuteronomy 30.1-3 for instance) — now God was to demonstrate it in the most amazing way. But the parable was not yet finished. The elder son was furious at the reception his brother received (vv.25-28) and told his father the reason in no uncertain terms (vv.29-30). His father's only response was to assure him that he, too, had his undying and open-handed love. The challenge to the Pharisees was obvious — as it should be obvious to us. There is no place for peevishness, envy, jealousy or pride in God's family. Let us rejoice at his goodness to others, and at his goodness to us, remembering that in neither case is it ever the result of merit on our part but always of mercy on his!

"The Lord God, merciful and gracious, longsuffering, and abundant in goodness and truth" (Exodus 34.6)

43
Money Matters (1)
Luke 16.1-13

The previous chapter of Luke's Gospel contained three well-known parables; this one contains two that are less familiar. The subject in Chapter 15 was God's love for sinners; here it is basically man's use of wealth. The first of these two parables is very difficult to understand with precision, but the following summary would fit the facts as we have them. A rich man received a report that his manager was swindling him (v.1)—possibly by adding a certain amount to loans on which interest was already being charged, and then pocketing the difference when the loans were repaid. Threatened with dismissal and unemployment (v.3) the manager hit on a crafty scheme to get the debtors on his side (v.4). Quickly summoning them one at a time, he authorised them to reduce the amounts they owed — amounts that were apparently payable in kind rather than in cash. For example, a man who owed "eight hundred gallons of olive oil" (v.6 NIV) was told to reduce it by half. Another man whose debt was valued at "a thousand bushels of wheat" (v.7 NIV) was told to call it 800. It was a brilliant move, because the debtors were now in his debt! What is more, if we have the outline of the story right, his master was also in some difficulty, as he was breaking the Old Testament law about lending money (see Exodus 22.25 for example). Unable to press the matter any further he "commended the dishonest manager because he had acted shrewdly" (v.8 NIV). From this whole murky business Jesus drew out four lessons about man's use of wealth.

A Lesson About Shrewdness Jesus commented on the remarkable shrewdness of ordinary, unconverted people "in dealing with their own kind" (v.8 NIV). While we must never imitate their dishonesty, it is a great loss to the kingdom of God when Christians are slipshod and careless about their use of time, gifts and possessions. Compare "the children of light" in v.8 with John 12.36 and Ephesians 5.8.

A Lesson About Sharing Jesus went on to say that we should use our "worldly wealth" in such a way that at the end of life we will be "welcomed into eternal dwellings" (v.9 NIV). Money given to evangelism and other Christian work will then be seen to have been an investment paying enormous and eternal dividends (notice what Jesus said at Matthew 6.20 and 19.21).

A Lesson About Stewardship This was brought home by one statement and two questions. The statement is very telling (v.10). A man's character is shown in everything he does, not just by the big things. Even little actions speak louder than words. The questions make a direct challenge. Basically, the first question (v.11) asks this: if we are deficient in the way we use an ordinary thing like money, how can we expect God to entrust us with "true riches"? The second question presses home the same principle from an entirely different angle. Everything we handle here on earth is really "someone else's property" (v.12 NIV)—see 1 Chronicles 29.14 and 1 Corinthians 6.19-20 for the owner's identity! If we handle these things badly, how can we expect to receive those everlasting riches promised to faithful stewards? (compare Matthew 25.23) Our temporary stewardship will determine our permanent ownership.

A Lesson About Servitude This is in verse 13. A servant was in fact a slave, completely owned by his master, to whom he owed total allegiance. But the principle extends beyond that particular relationship. Deep in his heart, a man can only be committed in one direction— towards God or away from him; and the man preoccupied with money cannot possibly be a man of God.

"Lay not up for yourselves treasures upon earth" (Matthew 6.19)

44
Money Matters (2)
Luke 16.14-31

This passage follows directly on from the end of our last study, in which Jesus told the story about the shrewd manager and then drew some challenging conclusions about man's use of wealth. The Pharisees to whom Jesus was speaking are bluntly described as "covetous and lovers of money" (v.14 AMP) and it is therefore no surprise to read that they "began to ridicule and sneer and scoff at him" (v.14 AMP). But that kind of behaviour is often just a smoke-screen to cover up the truth, and Jesus quickly exposed them as hypocrites. In particular, he pointed out that what is "highly valued among men"—that is, the accumulation of wealth regardless of how it is gained or how it is used — is "detestable in God's sight" (v.15 NIV, and see Jeremiah 22.13-15). He then underlined his statement in two ways.

A Principle About Life The Pharisees may have been furious at a "layman" like Jesus daring to teach God's law to them, the self-professed experts (see John 7.15 for instance — and the answer Jesus gave them in the following verse!) but Jesus calmly pointed out that while John the Baptist's preaching marked the end of the Old Testament era (v.16), God's moral law remained unchanged (v.17—a "tittle" was a little hook on some letters of the Hebrew alphabet). Throughout his ministry Jesus made it clear that he had not come to destroy the law, but to fulfil it (see Matthew 5.17). Jesus completed God's law; the Pharisees corrupted it. The matter of divorce was an example of this. The law allowed a man to divorce his wife under certain circumstances (Deuteronomy 24.1-4). But some people stretched these conditions to include things as trivial as the woman speaking to a strange man or ruining her husband's meal! Jesus swept all these ridiculous interpretations aside and underlined God's original intention for his people, namely the sanctity, security and permanence of the marriage bond (read v.18 together with Matthew 19.3-9 where Jesus shows the principle to go back before the law of Moses). The principles of honesty and charity are equally part of God's permanent law for a man's life.

A Parable About Death The parable concerns two men. One was wealthy and self-indulgent— he "revelled and feasted and made merry in splendour every day" (v.19 AMP). The other man was a beggar called Lazarus, tormented by hunger, disease and scavenging dogs (vv.20-21). But for all his poverty, the beggar obviously possessed the riches of living faith (see James 2.5) because when he died he went to heaven (v.22). The rich man, on the other hand, lived and died without God— and went to hell (vv.22-23). The extraordinary conversation he had with Abraham reveals that in hell a person is "in torments" (v.23); he can in some way "see" heaven (v.23); he longs for relief from his agony (v.24); he can remember his life on earth (v.25); he recognises the need for people on earth to hear the gospel (vv.27-28) and he knows that repentance is essential (v.30). But it is all too late— between heaven and hell there is "a great gulf fixed" (v.26) and there is no traffic between the two. Notice what Jesus said in Matthew 25.46. After death, *all* men are eternally secure— the righteous in heaven and the unrighteous in hell! And what was the rich man's damning sin? He indulged his own selfish appetite day after day and ignored a starving beggar on his doorstep. No story could illustrate more clearly that the Bible's teaching on man's use of wealth is meant to be taken seriously. Statements like those at Proverbs 21.13, James 4.17 and 1 John 3.17 are literally matters of life and death!

"Every man shall give as he is able" (Deuteronomy 16.17)

45
Teaching, Preaching and Healing
Luke 17.1-19

At the beginning of his public ministry, we are told that Jesus "went about all Galilee teaching...and preaching the gospel of the kingdom, and healing all manner of sickness and all manner of disease among the people" (Matthew 4.23). Now, after nearly three years, and with the shadow of his death growing larger every day, we find him still engaged up to the hilt in his God-ordained ministry. No wonder he was able to say what he did at John 17.4!

Teaching There are three pieces of teaching in the early part of this chapter. The first is about causing people to sin (vv.1-2, and compare Mark 9.42). In a fallen world, temptation is inevitable (v.1) but those who put temptation in other people's way face certain and terrible judgment (v.2). By "these little ones" Jesus probably meant all Christians, old as well as young—a beautiful example of his loving care for them. Compare Matthew 18.14 and Luke 12.32—and notice at 1 John 5.21 how John followed his Master's example. Next came teaching about forgiveness (vv.3-4). Sin is not to be treated lightly—if a man sins we must "solemnly tell him so and reprove him" (v.3 AMP). But if he repents we must forgive him. "Seven times in a day" does not mean that we count the number of times we forgive; it means we forgive until we lose count! Compare Matthew 18.21-22 —our forgiveness is to be governed by compassion not by computer! The third piece of teaching is about our duty to God (vv.7-10). In a nutshell, the lesson is that we can never claim to put God in our debt (v.10). Link up Psalm 96.8, Ecclesiastes 12.13, Matthew 5.48 and Mark 12.30. When we have exceeded these we will have exceeded our duty! Who can dare to lift his head in pride?

Preaching This came in response to a request from the disciples (v.5). The good news Jesus declared was amazing (v.6). Faith links our impotence to God's omnipotence, and when that is in operation, anything can happen — and to "mountains" as well as "trees" (see Matthew 17.20). Faith and victory are inseparable in the Christian life (see 1 John 5.14).

Healing The story of the miraculous healing of ten lepers (vv.11-19) is exclusive to Luke. The lepers were standing "afar off" because of long-established quarantine laws (see Leviticus 13.45-46)—notice that they had to shout in order to be heard (v.13). The story is told without comment, but there is an important lesson in it. Notice that in verse 14 Jesus told the lepers to go and show themselves to the priests (who were authorised to pronounce a cured leper "clean" — see Leviticus 14.1-32, and especially verse 7). His instructions must have seemed crazy if not cruel—after all, the men were still covered with leprosy—but the lepers did as they were told, and "as they went, they were cleansed" (v.14). Mark that carefully! Only when they exercised faith did the miracle happen. But now a sour note creeps into the story. Of the ten men healed, only one, a Samaritan, returned to give thanks to Jesus (v.16) and to praise God for his goodness (v.15). Jesus pointed this out by means of two questions (vv.17-18), but the incident only illustrates the truth that ingratitude towards God is the mark of most of humanity (see Romans 1.21). The grateful Samaritan received a further word from Jesus (v.19) — and it may be that he received the added and greater blessing of salvation (compare Mark 10.52).

"It is a good thing to give thanks unto the Lord" (Psalm 92.1)

46
The Coming Of The Kingdom Of God
Luke 17.20-37

The air was now full of rumour, discussion and speculation about "the kingdom of God"—and this was hardly surprising. The Old Testament had been full of statements and prophesies about it, not least in connection with the coming Messiah (see Isaiah 9.6-7); John the Baptist had declared "the kingdom of heaven is at hand" (Matthew 3.2); and Jesus himself had told one parable after another to illustrate its nature. Against this background, the Pharisees' question may have been perfectly natural and innocent (v.20). In any event, it resulted in a straightforward statement to them and more detailed teaching to the disciples.

The King And The Kingdom The reply Jesus gave the Pharisees (v.21) probably meant something like "the kingdom of God is in the midst of you", meaning that Jesus himself was the personification of the kingdom of God. Not only were the words he spoke and the life he lived utterly different from those of any other man (see John 7.46); his whole personality was a living revelation of God (link John 1.14 and Colossians 2.9). The Pharisees were so spiritually blind that they were searching for the kingdom while looking at the king.

False Kingdoms Jesus now turned to his disciples, and began by warning them of trouble to come. For himself, there would be suffering and rejection (v.25) when the powers of darkness would reign (look ahead to 22.53). For the disciples, things would get so difficult that they would "long to see even one of the days of the Son of man" (v.22 AMP and compare Matthew 9.14-15). At the same time there would be all kinds of false dawns, promising the kingdom of God without producing it (compare vv.21 and 23 with Mark 13.21-22). This prophecy had been repeatedly fulfilled over the years, and in many different ways. The kingdom of God is neither ecclesiastical, political nor social.

The Real Kingdom The best way to deal with all these counterfeits is to realise that when "the day of the Son of man" (Christ's return to the earth) occurs, there will be no dispute about it. It will be as dazzling and definite as a flash of lightning (v.24) and will have immediate and unmistakable results (vv.34-36). The righteous will be taken up to be with the Lord (see 1 Thessalonians 4.17), while the unrighteous will be left to despair, judgment and doom.

The Unexpected Kingdom The solemn challenge just given is made urgent by the fact that by its very suddenness, Christ's return will catch people unawares (vv.26-30). There is obviously nothing inherently sinful about the activities mentioned here, such as eating, drinking, marrying, buying, selling, planting and building; but the inference is that people will be wholly taken up with things like these. A man caught up with this world is not ready for the next one. Materialism is no preparation for judgment or for heaven. Colossians 3.1-4 points to a better way.

When The Kingdom Comes With the warning "Remember Lot's wife" (v.32) Jesus reminded his disciples of one person who was reluctant to leave her earthly possessions (the story is told in Genesis 19.1-28 — see especially vv.17 and 23-28). The true disciple will not think first of his possessions (v.31) nor even of his own life (v.33). All of this ties in exactly with what we saw earlier at 14.25-33. Verse 37 is notoriously difficult, and over the years nearly 60 explanations of it have been given. Jesus may have meant that when the earth is ready for final judgment, that judgment will inevitably come. The same terrible truth is stated at Revelation 14.15.

"You too, be patient and stand firm, because the Lord's coming is near" (James 5.8 NIV)

47
Man's Approach To God
Luke 18.1-17

At this point, Luke's narrative continues to read like a colourful magazine, in which apparently unconnected features are placed along-side each other by the editor. This is certainly true about the early part of this chapter, though there is some kind of connecting link if we see each of the three sections as teaching one important truth about man's approach to God, either in his primary need of salvation or of a subsequent need of help in answer to prayer. One word will crystallise each of the attitudes we need to have.

Persistence The purpose of the first parable in this chapter is stated simply and clearly (v.1). As he seemed to constitute a one-man court, the judge in the story was probably a Roman (Jewish courts had three judges). He was certainly godless and unscrupulous (v.2) as were many Roman judges at that time. A certain widow in the town "kept coming to him" (v.3 NIV) asking for justice in what seems to have been a long-standing dispute. The judge ignored her for a while (v.4) but eventually gave in "so that she won't eventually wear me out with her coming" (v.5 NIV). The lesson Jesus drew from the parable was by way of contrast. If even a corrupt judge is capable of granting justice, surely God will "bring about justice for his chosen ones" (v.7 NIV). This has the same kind of ring about it as the statement made at 11.13. Christians will always be in the minority (notice the rhetorical question in verse 8) but our heavenly Father is "the giving God" (James 1.5 AMP), and this is surely great encouragement to Christians to "cry out to him day and night" (v.7 NIV).

Penitence The purpose of the second parable is equally clear, as we are told in verse 9. It was spoken to condemn those who trusted in their own goodness. In the story, two men — a Pharisee and a tax-collector — went up to the temple to pray. But the Pharisee never got around to praying. He spent all his time boasting to God of his honesty, purity and generosity and his general moral superiority (vv.11-12). There is no reason to doubt that he was telling the truth, but his whole attitude was one of insufferable arrogance; in his own eyes he was head and shoulders above other men (v.11). The tax-collector, on the other hand was totally different, in words and actions. He stood "afar off", bowed his head, and beat upon his breast (a sign of grief — see 23.48). His only words were "God be merciful to me a sinner" (v.13). Literally, he used the phrase "*the* sinner", as if he was the worst sinner in the world (compare Paul's estimation of himself at 1 Timothy 1.15). But it was this man who went home "justified", that is, right with God — for the reason given at the end of verse 14. (Compare 14.11 and Matthew 23.12) The man who is not penitent cannot be pardoned (see Matthew 9.13).

Dependence The lovely little incident in verses 15-17 is also recorded by Matthew (19.13-15) and Mark (10.13-16), with minor differences in the wording. When some parents brought their babies to Jesus for his blessing, (v.15) the disciples protested, no doubt trying to protect Jesus from what they thought were unimportant matters. It is interesting to notice that whenever they did that kind of thing Jesus over-ruled them (see 18.39-40 and Matthew 15.23-24). Gladly welcoming the children, Jesus taught that a person could only receive the kingdom of God when he did so "as a little child" (v.17) — that is to say, in a spirit of unquestioning dependence on the goodness and mercy of God (notice how Jesus emphasised this at Matthew 18.1-3).

"It is good for me to draw near to God" (Psalm 73.28)

48
The Master At Work
Luke 18.18-43

At the end of his Gospel, the Apostle John says that if everything Jesus did while he was here on earth were written down "I suppose that even the whole world would not have room for the books that would be written" (John 21.25 NIV). That may be hyperbole, but it is impressive to notice how a small section of Luke's narrative such as today's reading contains a remarkable variety of work. We can get a general grasp of it by highlighting three particular things Jesus did.

The Failure He Revealed The "ruler" (v.18) — some kind of local official—asked a vitally important question —compare verse 18 with 10.25—but the most remarkable thing was the way he addressed Jesus. "*Good teacher*" (v.18 NIV) was an unheard-of phrase, as the Jews taught that only God and the law of God were wholly good. This helps to explain the opening words of Jesus' answer (v.19); the man was being challenged to consider the implication of what he said. As the ruler obviously thought he could be saved by his own goodness, Jesus pointed him to some of the commandments (v.20). Amazing as it may seem, the ruler believed that he had passed those tests (v.21). Without pausing to correct him, Jesus instantly revealed the man's basic flaw (vv.22-23); he put his goods before his God. When Jesus commented on the problems posed by wealth (compare vv.24-25 with 1 Timothy 6.9) the disciples were astonished (v.26)—not least because of a popular belief that wealth was a sign of God's favour. In reply, Jesus made a crucially important statement—link verse 27 with Galatians 2.16. No man, rich or poor, can ever achieve his own salvation; that power belongs exclusively to God. When Peter remarked that he and the other disciples had forsaken all to follow him (compare v.28 with 5.11), Jesus assured him that the Christian's rewards would always exceed his sacrifices, both in this life and in the life to come (vv.29-30, and see Mark 8.35).

The Forecast He Repeated It is sometimes forgotten that as well as being a king (John 18.37) and a priest (Hebrews 4.14) Jesus was also a prophet (link Deuteronomy 18.18 with Matthew 21.11) — and as a prophet he had authority both to forthtell and foretell God's word. In verses 31-33 he made another forecast of his coming death and resurrection (compare 9.22). For the first time he spoke of being handed over to "the Gentiles" (v.32) — a clear reference to the fact that the Romans would carry out his torture and execution. Notice the remarkable details given here — and check each one of them against Matthew 27.26-30. Yet all of these formed part of a vast body of prophecy extending right back through the Old Testament, all of which was to be fulfilled to the letter (v.31). The disciples were still baffled by it all (v.34) — but knowing, as we do, that they were fulfilled, these prophecies should help us to grasp the amazing authority and accuracy of the whole Bible.

The Faith He Rewarded The story of the healing of the blind man is vividly and dramatically told (vv.35-43). Perhaps the most outstanding thing to notice is the blind man's faith. Whereas the crowd explained the commotion to him by saying that "Jesus of Nazareth is passing by" (v.37 NIV), he cried out to him as "Jesus, Son of David" (v.38) — a title reserved exclusively for the Messiah (see Jeremiah 23.5). The blind man may not have realised all that this meant, but he fervently pinned his faith in the One whom he believed to be the Christ. God's promise is that that kind of faith will never go unrewarded (2 Chronicles 20.20) — and for the blind man it brought instant healing (v.42) for which he in turn gave all the glory to God (v.43).

"Our God whom we serve is able to deliver us" (Daniel 3.17)

49
From Jericho To Jerusalem (1)
Luke 19.1-27

Luke now begins to give us much more detail about the location of his narrative. The blind man was healed as Jesus approached Jericho (look back to 18.35); this new chapter begins with him passing through that city (v.1) which was about 20 miles from Jerusalem. By verse 29 he had reached Bethany, about 18 miles on; by verse 41 he was in sight of Jerusalem; and at verse 45 he entered the city which was to see the climax of his earthly life. In today's reading, Luke records just one extended incident, in which a rich man becomes a Christian and Jesus teaches a very serious lesson about Christian responsibility.

The Man Who Was Converted Jericho was a popular winter resort, an important trading centre, and world-famous for its balsam groves. Zaccheus is introduced as the "chief tax collector" (v.2 NIV)—the senior officer in what must have been a thriving department of the Civil Service in a wealthy town like Jericho. We are also told that he was rich — no doubt as the result of lining his pockets by fraud. Hearing that Jesus was in town, he was determined to see him, perhaps because he had heard that this remarkable preacher actually welcomed tax-collectors, whereas most people hated them like poison (see 15.1-2). As he was not tall enough to see over people's heads, he climbed up a sycamore tree (v.4). When Jesus arrived he called Zaccheus down and in-vited himself to his house (v.5). The crowd muttered their usual disapproval (v.7) but the effect on Zaccheus was instant and astonishing. In a moment of time he became "a new creation" (2 Corinthians 5.17 NIV). He obeyed Jesus immediately and welcomed him to his home (v.6). What is more, he announced his intention of giving half his possessions to charity and of repaying all the people he had swindled, with 300% interest! (v.8)—whereas even in a case of proven fraud the law only required the addition of 20% to the capital sum involved (see Numbers 5.5-7). No wonder Jesus was able to be so definite about Zaccheus's conversion! (v.9), declaring him a true, spiritual son of Abraham (see Galatians 3.6-7). Jesus added that it was precisely to carry out this kind of life-saving mission that he had come into the world (compare v.10 with 1 Timothy 1.15).

The Men Who Were Commended While the people were still listening, Jesus went on to tell them another parable, this time to correct the thinking of those who still hoped that he was about to set up an earthly kingdom at Jerusalem (v.11). As with all parables, we are not meant to squeeze every word until it produces a particular meaning, but rather to grasp the general picture and the main lessons. In this case, the main meaning comes across if we see the "nobleman" as representing Jesus, and the "ten servants" representing all Christians. In a nutshell, Jesus was teaching that though he would indeed "receive for himself a kingdom" (link v.12 with Revelation 17.14) he must first go into "a far country" (v.12) — that is, heaven (see John 14.1-2). In the meantime, his servants had work to do and in hostile surroundings (vv.13-14). When the nobleman returned, the servants who had been diligent were rewarded (vv.15-19), the one who had done nothing useful was impoverished (vv.20-24), and his rebellious enemies were destroyed (v.27). Christ has entrusted us with the stewardship of every gift we have, including the gospel itself (see 1 Thessalonians 2.4) and we are answerable to him for all we do (look up 2 Corinthians 5.10). Whether or not we receive the kind of reward mentioned in the parable will depend entirely on the quality of our stewardship (see 1 Corinthians 3.11-15).

"May our Lord Jesus Christ…and God our Father…encourage and strengthen you in every good deed and word" (2 Thessalonians 2.16-17 NIV).

50
From Jericho To Jerusalem (2)
Luke 19.28-46

After the story of Zaccheus's conversion, Luke tells us nothing else about Jesus' journey towards Jerusalem until he reaches Bethany, almost on the outskirts of the city. Here, Jesus seems to have put a pre-arranged plan into operation. He told two disciples to go ahead to the next village and bring back a young donkey they would find there (compare v.30 with Matthew 21.2). If questioned, they were to give a kind of password — "The Lord needs it" (v.31 NIV). Exactly as arranged, the donkey was brought (vv.32-35) and Jesus began the final two-mile journey into Jerusalem.

The Praise That Was Offered The annual Feast of the Passover was now approaching, and for Jesus to enter Jerusalem at a time when the authorities would be particularly alert showed great courage. There was an undisguised determination to kill him, and people doubted whether he would risk attending the Feast at all (see John 11.53-57). But Jesus knew that this was his God-ordained pathway, and he was determined to follow it (see 9.51). Not only did he enter the city openly, but his choice of transport was vividly significant. An Old Testament prophet had made it clear that Messiah would enter Jerusalem riding on a young donkey (see Zachariah 9.9) — and here was Jesus fulfilling that prophecy to the letter. When they pull all of this alongside the many miracles they had seen him perform (v.37) the crowds went wild with delight, even shouting words from a Messianic Psalm to express their feelings (link v.38 with Psalm 118.26). When some of the Pharisees told him to put a stop to all of this, Jesus told them that nothing could hold back the acclamation which was rightly due to him (vv.39-40). Although he knew that much of it was superficial, Jesus accepted his worship by the people as his Divine right (see Philippians 2.9-11).

The Pain That Was Felt But in the middle of this triumphant day Jesus suddenly broke down in tears (v.41). The cause of his sorrow was because he knew what would follow Jerusalem's spiritual blindness and her failure to respond to his message (v.42 and the end of v.44). The prophecy he made (vv.43-44) was literally fulfilled in AD 70 when Jerusalem was first besieged and then destroyed by Roman armies, resulting in a terrible massacre that could have been avoided had the Jews followed his peaceful pathways rather than their own hotheaded ideas (link v.42 with 1.79). But there is a wider fulfilment of this prophecy which the Bible applies to all those who reject the reign of Christ and his gracious gospel invitation. Paul spells it out in the solemn words of 2 Thessalonians 1.7-9.

The Purging That Was Needed Soon after his arrival in the city (Mark tells us that it was on the following day—see Mark 11.11-15) Jesus went into the temple area and drove out the traders selling sacrificial animals (v.45) and, as Mark tells us, overturned the tables of the money-changers (Mark 11.15). Under the Jewish religious system both facilities would have been very helpful, but many of the operators were notoriously dishonest, and that kind of thing going on within the temple precincts drove Jesus to take drastic action. It is surprising not to read of a violent reaction by the authorities—but perhaps the reason is that Jesus was able to enlist their cherished Old Testament prophets in defence of his action (compare v.46 with Isaiah 5.6-7 and Jeremiah 7.11).

"A false balance is abomination to the Lord" (Proverbs 11.1)

51
Questions And Answers (1)
Luke 19.47-20.19

Jesus had now entered the last week of his earthly life, and the scene was being set for its dramatic climax. He was in Jerusalem, the very headquarters of enemies bent on his destruction (19.47). Yet he went fearlessly on, going openly to the temple area every day, "teaching the people … and preaching the gospel" (20.1 NIV). These days are covered by Luke in the next two chapters (look ahead to 21.37-38). Much more must have been said than has been recorded, but we can learn important lessons from the teaching preserved for us here, much of it sparked off by questions put to Jesus.

The Authority Of Jesus The first question came from "the chief priests and the teachers of the law" (v.1 NIV) —the religious experts—and we can understand why they put their double-barrelled challenge (v.2). After all, Jesus had swept into the temple area, disrupting things left, right and centre. Who did he think he was? Notice, incidentally, that they sent a team to investigate John the Baptist in a similar way when he burst on the scene a few years earlier (John 1.19-22). Rather than give a direct reply, Jesus asked a question about John's ministry (vv.3-4). Now they were cornered! Whilst they had rejected John, he had been very popular with the people (see Matthew 3.5). More importantly, John had clearly said that he was preparing the way for Jesus, whom he called "the Son of God" (see John 1.29-34). Now if they acknowledged that John was a genuine prophet sent from God, they would be condemned for rejecting him —and for rejecting his testimony about Jesus (v.5); on the other hand, they were afraid to disown John in case of a violent reaction by the crowd (v.6) — compare Herod's dilemma at Matthew 14.5. In the end, they pretended that they were incapable of coming to a decision on the matter (v.7). Jesus refused to trade words with such hypocritical liars (v.8). He was under no obligation to answer dishonest questions.

Jesus And The Authorities Jesus now turned to the crowd (v.9) and told them a parable which both answered the original question and condemned those who rejected it. The story itself is simple enough (vv.9-16), but the obvious interpretation infuriated the religious leaders (v.19). They would have remembered the same kind of picture used by one of the great Old Testament prophets (read Isaiah 5.1-7) — and they would have no difficulty in identifying the items and people in the parable. The "man" was God; the "vineyard" was Israel; they themselves, and their predecessors, were the "husbandmen" (tenants); the "servants" were the prophets; and the "beloved son" was Jesus. Everything fitted perfectly! — even though the crowd was aghast at the thought of the kingdom of God being given to "others" (v.16) — which could only mean the inclusion of Gentiles. Jesus now drove home the point about his authority by quoting from the very Psalm the crowd had used in welcoming him into the city (link v.17 with Psalm 118.22). Peter applied the same quotation to Jesus more than once—see Acts 4.11 and 1 Peter 2.7-8—and of course the issue is crucial. Notice how solemnly Jesus put this in verse 18. If a person strikes himself against Christ in opposition or unbelief he will hurt himself badly (compare Isaiah 45.9); and if the day comes when Christ falls on him in judgment, he will be utterly destroyed.

"God has made ... Jesus ... both Lord and Christ" (Acts 2.36 NIV)

52

Questions And Answers (2)
Luke 20.20-40

By now, the enemies of Jesus were watching him like hawks, looking for an opportunity to have him killed, (see 19.47). But with amazing courage, Jesus continued to teach quite openly. Today's reading contains two questions and the answers Jesus gave to them.

The Matter Of Taxation As their direct attacks had failed, the enemies of Jesus now sent spies into the front line (v.20). These were not themselves scribes or Pharisees, but some of their students (compare Matthew 22.16). They began with a hefty dose of flattery (v.21). Neither they nor their masters believed a word of this. It was just a crude device to give the impression of being honest men who recognised truth when they heard it. Then came their carefully worded question (v.22). No doubt infuriated that Jesus had placed them in a quandary (v.4) they felt that this would put him in an even worse dilemma. The "tribute" was a personal tax levied by the Romans. It amounted to just a few pence a year, but had to be paid in Roman currency. The coin used was the silver denarius, which bore the head of the Emperor and words which virtually described him as a divine ruler. It therefore caused great offence to the Jews (see Acts 5.36-37). The dilemma was this: if Jesus said it was wrong to pay tax he would be arrested by the Romans; if he said it was right, he would offend his Jewish followers. But Jesus saw straight through the trick. He took a denarius and asked "whose portrait and inscription are on it?" (v.24 NIV). When they told him "Caesar's" he laid down a masterly principle (v.25). To use Caesar's coins was to acknowledge his authority, and to accept an obligation to pay what was legally due to him. We have a duty to pay for the privileges our government and society provide (see

Romans 13.1-7). But where the law of man and the law of God conflict, our duty is equally clear (see Acts 5.27-29). God has the greater kingdom and the prior claim (see Daniel 4.34). In the face of such precise yet perfect wisdom, the spies were silenced (v.26).

The Matter Of Resurrection The Sadducees were a sect who did not believe in angels, spirits or resurrection (compare v.27 with Acts 23.8). They also treated the books of Moses (Genesis-Deuteronomy) as superior to the rest of the Old Testament. They now came to Jesus, quoted Moses (link v.28 with Deuteronomy 25.5-6) recited an unlikely story (vv.29-32) and asked a question (v.33). They probably argued that as this would produce a ridiculous situation, the whole idea of resurrection could be dismissed. In reply, Jesus said two basic things. Firstly, even their great hero, Moses, had implied that the dead rise again, as he had spoken of the God of Abraham, Isaac and Jacob (link v.37 with Exodus 3.6). Surely God was the God of these men as living beings, and not just as piles of bones? (v.38) Secondly, in their resurrected state, people "are like the angels" in that "they can no longer die" (v.36 NIV). As there is no death in heaven, there is no need for birth, and therefore no need for marriage. The Sadducees' question was therefore a monumental irrelevance. Matthew 22.29 exposes it in another way! The Bible does not give us a detailed description of life in heaven, and we dare not try to fill in the gaps. Yet what we *are* told is surely enough to make Christians long for that day when in the fullest sense they shall know the experience of being "the children of God" (v.36, and compare 1 John 3.2).

"(The body) is sown in dishonour, it is raised in glory" (1 Corinthians 15.43 NIV)

53
Questions And Answers (3)
Luke 20.41-21.4

Today's reading is our third in Luke's coverage of the teaching Jesus gave in Jerusalem during the week leading up to his death. This passage covers three distinct and unrelated sections.

A Lesson About Prophecy The answer Jesus had given to the Sadducees about the doctrine of resurrection had put paid to any further questions (see v.40). The scribes (teachers of the law) took some satisfaction from this particular exchange, for there was little love lost between them and the Sadducees. But they had hardly finished congratulating Jesus on his victory (v.39) before he challenged them with questions of his own. Matthew tells us that he first asked whose son (that is, descendant) they thought the Christ (the Messiah) was (see Matthew 22.42). They had no problem in answering "David's". The Old Testament stated it (see 2 Samuel 7.12-13) and they themselves taught it (see John 7.42, for instance). That explains the question Luke records (vv.41 and 44). In between the questions, Jesus quoted the opening verse of Psalm 110 (vv.42-43), and said that David was speaking about the Messiah (compare Acts 2.34-35 and 1 Corinthians 15.25). But David had referred to the Messiah not as "my Son" but as "my Lord". Jesus' second question therefore meant "How then can Messiah merely be David's physical descendant?" Nobody could answer that (see Matthew 22.46) and Jesus left it there. For the moment, he wanted to make just one point clear — Christ was not only David's descendant, he was his Lord and God; not just his successor but his Sovereign. He would add the final truth later (see Matthew 26.63-64, and compare Romans 1.3). When it comes to the person of Jesus, there is no identity crisis in the Bible!

A Lesson About Hypocrisy Throughout his ministry, Jesus reserved some of his most withering attacks for the sin of hypocrisy. He now singled out the scribes for particular attention. They loved to project themselves as being both pious and important (v.46). But even their long-winded prayers were insincere, and just "for a show" (v.47). Underneath, they were self-centred and greedy, and would even wheedle extravagant personal gifts out of helpless widows in the name of religion. Jesus bluntly promised that "such men will be punished most severely" (v.47 NIV). The person who reads these words should examine his actions and motives with very great care!

A Lesson About Generosity Part of the temple area was The Court of the Women, which contained thirteen collecting-boxes shaped like upturned trumpets. It was into one of these boxes that Jesus saw certain rich people placing their gifts (v.1). He then saw a very poor widow put in "two mites" (v.2). The "mite" (also mentioned at 12.59) was the *lepton,* the smallest Jewish coin of all. Yet Jesus said that this widow put in "more than all the others" (v.3 NIV). Why? Because the others had given a token of their plenty, whereas she had given the total of her poverty (v.4). Few things test a Christian's spirituality better than the way he uses money. The Bible teaches us that we are to give willingly (1 Chronicles 29.9), proportionately (Deuteronomy 16.17) generously (Matthew 10.8) and worshipfully (Proverbs 3.9). Check these carefully and take an honest look at your standard of giving.

"He who has a bountiful eye shall be blessed" (Proverbs 22.9 RSV)

54

Troubles And Triumph To Come (1)

Luke 21.5-19

The setting for the main part of this remarkable chapter comes at the very end, where Luke tells us the daily routine Jesus followed (look ahead to vv.37-38). As Jesus was leaving the temple one afternoon, some of the disciples commented on its great beauty (v.5). To their amazement, Jesus said that the day was coming when it would be razed to the ground (v.6). When they reached the Mount of Olives, four of them asked him when this would happen and what the warning signs would be (v.7, and read March 13.1-4 for details omitted by Luke). These two questions led Jesus into a remarkable series of prophecies relating to the destruction of Jerusalem, the end of the world and his own personal return to the earth. Most of the chapter is taken up with signs and warnings, but there are also words of encouragement and the promise of the ultimate triumph of God and his people. Today's reading is generally concerned with the fall of Jerusalem, and Jesus outlines three ways in which, before that happened, the Christians' faith would be tested.

Deception In a previous prophecy about the end of the world, Jesus had warned his disciples about people who would make supernatural claims (look back to 17.20-23); now he underlined the same thing (v.8). There is an example of this kind of thing happening at Acts 8.9-10. The disciples' instructions in this kind of situation were crystal clear — "do not follow them" (v.8 NIV). Some religious and philosophical leaders make similar claims today; the Christians' instructions have not changed!

Disruption Jesus next prophesied that there would be a breakdown in international relationships (v.10)—something later recorded by reliable historians. Then there would be disruption both on the earth and in the sky (v.11). The historian Josephus records one of these "great signs from heaven" (v.11 NIV) — a comet in the shape of a sword which hung pointed over Jerusalem for a whole year. Signs like these must have terrified many people; it was typically gracious of Jesus to prepare his people for them, so that they need be neither surprised nor terrified.

Detestation But there was more personal trouble ahead for the Christians, and Jesus now told them what that would be. Because of their faith, they would be persecuted and put on trial by both Jews — in "the synagogues"—and Gentiles—"kings and rulers" (v.12). Worse still, some would be betrayed by members of their own families (v.16). The seeds of this warning had been sown earlier — see 12.52-53 — now the full truth must be told. Yet out of all of this hatred, bitterness and cruelty, a great deal of good would come. Firstly, their arrest and trial would give Christians an opportunity to bear witness for Christ (v.13, and notice what Paul said at Philippians 1.12-14). Secondly, in these moments of crisis Jesus promised that he would give them "words and wisdom that none of your adversaries will be able to resist or contradict" (v.15 NIV). Compare this with what Jesus had said earlier (12.11-12) — and notice how exactly this promise was fulfilled in the case of Stephen (Acts 6.10). Thirdly, although some of them would be put to death (v.16) none of them would come to any harm! (v.18) As we saw earlier, even the power of a godless executioner is strictly limited! (12.4) As God's children, they were eternally secure in his loving hands; and they would gain everything by "steadfastness and patient endurance" (v.19 AMP). These promises must have been a tremendous comfort to those first disciples. The principles they contain are no less precious to those who faithfully seek to follow Christ today.

"The angel of the Lord encamps around those who fear him, and delivers them" (Psalm 34.7 RSV).

55

Troubles And Triumph To Come (2)

Luke 21.20-38

Today's reading continues the remarkable series of prophecies, warnings and instructions which Jesus gave in answer to the disciples' original questions about the forthcoming destruction of Jerusalem (v.7). In this closing section, Jesus specifically deals with the fall of the city, but then widens his comments to include events to take place at his second coming and the end of the world.

The Terrible Ruin Of Jerusalem The final sign that the city's destruction was near would be that hostile troups would begin to surround it (link v.20 with 19.43). From then on, the city's doom was inevitable, both as a punishment and as a fulfilment of prophecy (link v.22 with 19.44). There would therefore be no point in heroic resistance. The Christians should get out — quickly! (v.21) The historian Eusebius says that the Christians in the city when the siege began (AD 70) did exactly as they had been instructed and escaped across the river Jordan to the city of Pella. It was as well that they did, because the terrible savagery which Jesus prophesied in vv.23-24 then fell on the doomed city. One historian speaks of over 1,000,000 people killed and 97,000 young men taken into captivity; not one Jew was left alive in the whole city! From then on, Jerusalem was "trampled on by the Gentiles" (v.24) for one century after another. The phrase "until the times of the Gentiles be fulfilled" may mean something like "until the Gentiles have had all of the full opportunity God intends them to have to respond to the gospel". Speculation as to when that might be is both foolish and futile.

The Triumphant Return Of Jesus From verse 25 on-wards, Jesus seems to be referring to the events surrounding his second coming (notice vv.27 and 36). As with the fall of Jerusalem, Christ's return will be preceded by spectacular and fearful happenings. Compare vv.25-36 with vv.10-11 and notice that both sections include upheavals on the earth and extraordinary phenomena in the sky. Notice, too, what is said at 2 Peter 3.10-12. Not surprisingly, Jesus said that men would "faint from terror, apprehensive of what is coming on the world" (v.26 NIV)—but Christians are to "stand up" and lift up their heads (v.28 NIV). Their confidence is to be based on the kind of certainty illustrated by Jesus in a tiny parable (vv.29-30). These terrible events would mean that two things, both closely connected, were very near—the kingdom of God and the Christians' full and final redemption (vv.31 and 28). Notice how Paul uses the same comforting truth that for Christians living on earth, salvation is something in the future, but drawing nearer all the time (Romans 13.11). Jesus next went on to say that however appalling their persecution, the Jewish race would survive until the end of time (this is the probable meaning of v.32). All of these things were guaranteed by the fact that Christ's words were indestructible (v.33)—as is all of God's word (look back to 16.17 and compare Isaiah 40.8 and 1 Peter 1.24-25). Having given such a full and loving warning, Jesus went on to say that the actual day of his return would come as suddenly as a trap being sprung (v.34, and look back to 17.24 for another illustration Jesus used to say the same thing). That being so, Christians should be "always on the watch" (v.36 NIV). In particular, they should avoid "dissipation, drunkenness and the anxieties of life" (v.34 NIV). Selfish indulgence in pleasure or self-centered preoccupation with work is poor preparation for the Lord's return. If these warnings were true when they were first spoken, they are nearly 2,000 years more urgently true today!

"Everyone who has this hope in him purifies himself" (1 John 3.3 NIV).

56
The Last Supper (1)
Luke 22.1-23

With the end of the last chapter, Luke came to the close of his account of Christ's public ministry. Now he moves on to the events surrounding his death. In the opening part of this chapter, three key things are mentioned, the last two blending together in a remarkable way.

A Record Of Judas's Defection Judas Iscariot is one of the most tragic figures in the whole Bible. Called to be a follower of Jesus (see Matthew 10.4) he moved so intimately in the disciples' circles that he became the group's treasurer (see John 13.29). But he misused his office and swindled the others by stealing money from the funds (see John 12.6). Now, he did something infinitely worse; he went to the authorities and suggested that he should betray Jesus (v.4). We are not told why he did such an appalling thing, but perhaps he was disgusted that he was not, after all, going to share in the glory of an earthly kingdom set up by Jesus. Needless to say, money was involved (v.5) and we are told elsewhere that the price agreed was "thirty pieces of silver" (see Matthew 26.14-15). Shamefully, this was the amount of compensation a man would have to pay if his ox gored another man's slave (see Exodus 21.32); amazingly, it was the exact amount prophecied over 500 years earlier! (look up Zechariah 11.12-13). Judas managed to cover up his plot very skilfully (vv.21-23)—but he would eventually have to pay a terrible price (v.22). Judas stands as a terrible warning that neither mixing with other Christians nor holding office in the church is any guarantee of a man's salvation. Although he was often *at* Christ's side, Judas was never really *on* Christ's side (see John 13.10-11), and the devil was able to use him at will (link v.3 with John 6.70).

111

A Reminder Of The Jews' Deliverance The Jewish Feast of Unleavened Bread was loosely called The Passover (v.1) though in fact they were two separate events celebrated at the same time. The Passover commemorated the deliverance of the Jews after 430 years captivity in Egypt (see Exodus 12, especially vv.14, 24-27 and 40-42). The Feast of Unleavened Bread was another simple yet vivid reminder of the same marvellous event in their history (see Exodus 12.15-20 and 13.3-10). No faithful Jew would fail to carry out these clear instructions. Continual gratitude for all the Lord's goodness is a sure mark of spirituality (see 1 Thessalonians 5.18); forgetfulness of his kindness is always a dangerous sign (see Jeremiah 3.21).

A Representation Of Jesus's Death As they reclined at table, Jesus told the disciples how much he had looked forward to this special meal (v.15) but that this would be the last Passover he would celebrate with them on earth (vv.16 and 18). During a normal Passover meal, those taking part would share three cakes of unleavened bread and drink from four cups of wine. Jesus now took these familiar things and used them as symbols of his forthcoming death (vv.19-20). In particular, he said that his death would establish a new covenant for his people (as prophesied at Jeremiah 31.31-34). Then, in the simplest possible way, he instructed his disciples to continue this simple ceremony as a permanent reminder of his death on their behalf (link vv.19-20 with 1 Corinthians 11.23-26). We cannot be sure how much of this the disciples fully understood at the time, but within a few years, the Lord's Supper, as it became known, had replaced the Passover ceremony as far as Christians were concerned. Ever since, it has been a sacred and solemn reminder of our Saviour's death (see 1 Corinthians 10.16-17).

"Christ our Passover is sacrificed for us: therefore let us keep the feast" *(1 Corinthians 5.7-8).*

57

The Last Supper (2)
Luke 22.24-38

In today's reading, Luke continues his account of the last Passover meal Jesus had with his disciples, a meal which he turned into the first Lord's Supper (or Holy Communion), the symbol of the new covenant which he was shortly to establish with his own blood (see Hebrews 13.20). The pieces of conversation which Luke records, focussing on the teaching Jesus gave, can be grouped into three paragraphs.

The Pride He Condemned It seems pathetic that with Jesus speaking so movingly about his death (now only a few hours away) the disciples should still be arguing about which of them should be "considered to be the greatest" (v.24 NIV). They had done this kind of thing before (see Mark 9.33-35) but they had obviously not learned the lesson Jesus taught them on that occasion. Jesus now condemned their attitude as downright worldly — the kind of thing godless kings did. Some Syrian and Egyptian kings actually took the title of "Benefactor" to draw attention to their authority; which explains the reference in verse 25. Jesus then went on to say that Christian behaviour should be exactly the opposite (v.26). The love of titles, prestige and authority are wrong in the world and worse in the church — and Christians with gifts which make them candidates for leadership should examine their motives with particular and honest care (link Jeremiah 45.5 with 1 Peter 5.2-3). As Jesus had pointed out earlier, there are inflexible laws governing this whole area (check Mark 9.35 again). What is more, he himself was the perfect illustration of the principles he laid down. In Old Testament prophecy he was described as a "servant" (Isaiah 42.1); speaking of his own life he said that "the Son of Man did not come to be served, but to serve" (Mark 10.45 NIV); John tells us that at the Last Supper Jesus actually washed the disciples' feet (John 13.3-4); and Paul puts into one stupendous statement the Saviour's greatest act of humility — and his greatest honour as a result! (Philippians 2.5-11).

The Privilege He Conferred Jesus next went on to tell the disciples that as those who had been faithful to him, they were all to be given a kingdom (v.29), in the sense that they would share in his honour, joy and glory of his own eternal reign (v.30). The phrase "judging the twelve tribes of Israel" may be a symbolic way of expressing this. The disciples were squabbling over who should be chairman, while Jesus was promising them that they would be kings! Check your own earthly ambitions in the light of 1 Peter 1.3-5.

The Pressure He Considered But all of this was in the future. Before that, there were pressures to face, and Jesus now considered these. He told Peter that Satan had asked (God) for permission to test the disciples very seriously (compare v.31 with Job 1.6-12 and 2.1-7). The inference then seems to be that the disciples would crack under pressure, but that Peter, although he, too, would waver badly, would help them to recover their faith (vv.32-34). Incidentally, notice how these verses indicate Christ's diety — no mere man could possibly have known all these things. Finally, Jesus then warned them to prepare for the next, more difficult phase of their lives. Thus far, there had been special provision for their brief bursts of evangelistic activity (v.35); from now on, they would need to make sensible provision for their maintenance and defence (v.36). Misunderstanding his reference to buying swords, they told Jesus that they had two already (v.38). In reply Jesus said "That is enough" (v.38 NIV) — obviously not meaning that two would be sufficient to defend eleven men against all their enemies, but rather that they should stop using such aggressive and militant language. The kingdom of God is not won by a military campaign.

"The weapons we fight with are not the weapons of the world" *(2 Corinthians 10.4 NIV).*

58
Despised And Rejected
Luke 22.39-71

About 700 years before he came to earth, it was prophesied of Jesus that he would be "despised and rejected of men; a man of sorrows and acquainted with grief" (Isaiah 53.3). The terrible truth of all that this means now begins to unfold.

Agony When the Last Supper was over, Jesus went with the disciples to the Mount of Olives (v.39). Here, he left the disciples for a while to pray alone (v.41). His prayer was simple, yet tremendously profound and we are on holy ground in trying to grasp its full meaning (v.42). Because he was truly human he naturally shrank from the terrible death which faced him the next morning; so he prayed that God should deliver him from it "if you are willing". Yet because his will was totally submitted to the will of God, he added "yet not my will, but yours be done" (v.42 NIV). Here is a model prayer, showing that God constantly requires our submission to his sovereignty (compare Matthew 6.10). Even with the comfort of an angel (v.43) the agony of the experience was so great for Jesus that blood oozed from his pores and mingled with the sweat that dripped from his face.

Treachery Meantime, the disciples had been asleep "exhausted from sorrow" (v.45 NIV). Later, as Jesus was talking to them, Judas appeared with a mob armed with swords and clubs (link v.47 with Matthew 26.47). To prevent a wrongful arrest, Judas had arranged to identify Jesus with a kiss (link the end of v.47 with Matthew 26.48). The disciples were all for fighting it out (v.49) and one of them — John tells us it was Peter (see John 18.10) — had actually slashed a man's ear off before being told "No more of this!" (vv. 50-51 NIV — and compare this with v.38). Turning to the crowd, Jesus inferred that even the timing of his arrest was God-ordained (vv.52-53).

Tragedy Jesus was taken straight to the house of the high priest, Peter following "at a distance" (v.54 NIV). The other disciples had run away (see Mark 14.50), and Peter's personal tragedy was soon to follow. While Jesus was on trial for his life, Peter was on trial for his loyalty (vv.55-59). Though he was positively identified, and his accent proved he was a Galilean (v.59) he flatly denied that he knew Jesus at all. Just as he lied for the third time, the cock crowed (v.60). One look from Jesus was enough to remind Peter of what he had said a few hours earlier (link v.61 with 22.34). Peter "went out and wept bitterly" (v.62) but they were tears of repentance, and they marked the beginning of the way back. It is the man with no tears for his sin who is to be pitied.

Mockery When this first trial was over, Jesus was left in the custody of the guards, who mocked him, beat him, spat in his face (link v.63 with Matthew 26.67) and even played a crude game of Blind Man's Buff with him (v.64). Yet even this mockery was a fulfillment of prophecy (see Isaiah 50.6).

"Blasphemy" The examination before the high priest was not strictly legal, as no trial on a charge carrying the death penalty was allowed at night. So at the crack of dawn, the council (or Sanhedrin) was hurriedly assembled. When they asked Jesus if he was the Christ (the Messiah) he told them that their question was insincere (vv.67-68) then added a statement that prompted an even more dramatic question (vv.69 70). To that, Jesus replied "You are right in saying I am" (v.70 NIV). That made it an open and shut case as far as the council was concerned. This was downright blasphemy (compare 5.21) for which there was only one penalty (link v.71 with Matthew 26.65-66). But Jesus was not prepared to save his life at the expense of the truth.

"This is my beloved Son, in whom I am well pleased" (Matthew 3.17).

59
Countdown To Calvary
Luke 23.1-25

The trial by the Sanhedrin had been a farce because the members had decided on their verdict before the trial began! (read John 11.47-53) But they were still not able to carry out the death penalty (see John 18.31). That power lay with the Romans, who would not be interested in Jewish religious law. Some kind of political charge was needed. Luke now continues his story.

Malevolence Thirsting for blood, "the whole assembly rose and led (Jesus) off to Pilate" (v.1 NIV). The three new charges they laid against him (note these at v.2) were all maliciously untrue (for example, contrast the second charge with 20.25!). Taken together, they accused Jesus of being a political agitator. From Pilate's examination of Jesus, Luke records only one question (v.3). The reply he received (v.3) obviously satisfied Pilate that Jesus was no threat whatever to Roman security, and he passed a verdict of Not Guilty (v.4). The council was furious, and insisted that Jesus had caused trouble all the way from Galilee. The mention of Galilee gave Pilate an idea, because it came under the control of Herod Antipas, who was then in Jerusalem. Pilate jumped at the chance to evade any further responsibility, and by showing that he recognised Herod's jurisdiction he would help to patch up a quarrel that existed between them (vv.6-7 and 12). But was this yet another fulfilment of prophecy? — look at Psalm 2.2-3.

Silence Herod was delighted. It would be great fun to have a close look at this fellow, especially if he turned on a miracle or two. (link v.8 with 9.9) But in one of the most dreadful phrases in the Bible we read that Jesus "gave him no answer" (v.9 NIV). What a solemn warning to those who treat God in a casual or trivial way!

Nothing is more terrible than God's silence. Frustrated and angry, Herod responded by joining the soldiers in poking fun at Jesus before sending him back to Pilate (v.11).

Innocence Pilate began by reminding everyone that neither he nor Herod could find Jesus guilty of any capital offence (vv.13-15). Clearly wanting to let him go, he suggested a compromise. Perhaps a good beating would teach Jesus a lesson and he could then be released (v.16). The release could take place under special arrangement (see v.17 which has been inserted from Mark 15.6). This prisoner was chosen by popular demand, and Pilate offered the crowd two candidates—Jesus and Barabbas, a murderous rebel (read vv.18-19 with Matthew 27.15-17). When the crowd asked for the release of Barabbas, Pilate "appealed to them again" (v.20 NIV) but this only seemed to make things worse, for the crowd now started screaming for Jesus to be crucified (v.21). Pilate made one final appeal, again offering to beat Jesus before releasing him (v.22)—but by now the mob was in full cry. One man had nothing to say—see 1 Peter 2.23.

Sentence Luke's report of the sentence is concise and chilling — Pilate simply gave in to the mob (v.25). Yet neither Pilate nor the mob was in control. Jesus himself had already made it clear that he would be mocked, scourged and crucified (see Matthew 20.17-19). Little did Pilate and the mob know that as Jesus was led away, it was their hands that were tied, not his!

"This man was handed over ... by God's set purpose and foreknowledge" (Acts 2.23 NIV)

60
Last Words
Luke 23.26-56

We come now to the climax of all that has gone before—
the death of Jesus. In today's study we shall simply
concentrate on the last words of Jesus as recorded by
Luke (Matthew, Mark and John mention others).

The Word Of Sorrow As Jesus began the journey to the
place of execution, a great crowd followed, including
women from Jerusalem who "mourned and wailed for
him" (v.27 NIV) — sensing, perhaps, that there had
been a terrible miscarriage of justice. In a moment of
superb selflessness, Jesus turned and said that they
should be weeping for themselves and for their children
(v.28). He was obviously thinking of the coming destruction of Jerusalem, when it would be better to be childless
than to see one's children slaughtered (v.29). On that
day, people would want the earth to swallow them up
(link v.30 with Hosea 10.8). Verse 31 is a proverb which
probably meant "If they do this to someone who is
innocent, what will they do to the guilty?" Notice what is
said at 1 Peter 4.17-18.

The Word Of Sympathy Jesus had already told his
followers to love their enemies and pray for their perse-
cutors (see Matthew 5.43-44). Now, he proved that this
was no empty idealism, for as he hung on the cross,
naked and bleeding, he prayed "Father forgive them,
for they do not know what they are doing" (v.34 NIV).
The Romans certainly had no idea they were fulfilling
prophecy! (Link vv.33-34 with Psalm 22.16 and 18).

The Word Of Salvation Two common criminals were
being executed at the same time as Jesus (v.32) and they
now began cursing him (see Matthew 27.44). One of
them kept on arguing that if he was the Christ he ought

to save all three of them — but a remarkable change came over the other man. Suddenly, he rebuked his fellow criminal for insulting Jesus, admitted his own sin, acknowledged that Jesus was innocent, and the ruler of a spiritual kingdom beyond the grave, and cried to him for mercy! (vv.40-42). His repentance and faith were clearly genuine, because Jesus promised that he would be in heaven with him that very day (v.43). This beautiful word of salvation is a marvellous illustration of Romans 10.13.

The Word Of Surrender The very last words of Jesus on the cross, as recorded by Luke, are gentle, simple, but remarkable — "Father, into your hands I commit my spirit" (v.46 NIV). With his faculties crystal clear he placed his spirit into his Father's hands and laid down his life. Check how perfectly this agrees with John 10.17-18! Jesus is the only man in history who chose to die. His unique death was marked in several extraordinary ways (vv.44-45, and see others at Matthew 27.50-53). The "veil of the temple" was a huge curtain separating the people from the symbolic presence of God in the Holy of Holies. The tearing of this curtain could only mean one thing (see Hebrews 10.19-22). Luke then describes the impression made on the soldier in charge of the execution squad and on the people in general (vv.47-48). He also briefly records the burial of Jesus (vv.50-54) and tells us that certain women from Galilee made a note of where the body lay so that, when the Sabbath was over, they could complete the normal Jewish custom of embalming the dead body (vv.55-56). Of the death and burial of Jesus there could be no possible doubt.

"He ... became obedient to death — even death on a cross!" (Philippians 2.8 NIV)

61
Life After Death
Luke 24.1-32

Nothing has ever fascinated man more deeply than the question of whether there is life after death; and no man has ever examined the question properly until he has read the New Testament record of the events which followed the crucifixion of Jesus. Luke's last chapter is a vital part of that record.

The Empty Tomb The Jewish day began and ended at sunset, which meant that the Sabbath ended on our Saturday evening. It was therefore very early on the Sunday morning, "the first day of the week" that several women — some of them are mentioned in verse 10 — went to the grave to embalm the body of Jesus (v.1). They were amazed to find no body (vv.2-3). As they were thinking this through, they were startled by "two men in clothes that gleamed like lightning" (v.4 NIV) who suddenly stood beside them (later identified as angels—v.23). The women were naturally terrified but were immediately challenged with a question that went far beyond their feelings (v.5). Then came the most dramatic announcement in all history, "He is not here; he has risen!" (v.6 NIV) The angel then reminded them of what Jesus himself had promised (compare v.7 with 9.22). The women remembered perfectly well (v.8), which made their actions that morning a strange mixture of devotion and doubt. They had come to anoint the body of One who had said he would no longer be dead! So much of our sorrow today is because we fail to trust God's Word. Confused and embarrassed, the women hurried back to tell the other disciples, but "their words seemed to them like nonsense" (v.11 NIV). Just to doublecheck, Peter immediately ran to the grave where he found nothing except the strips of linen in which the body had been wrapped. The women were right! — and Peter had some thinking to do! (v.12).

The Risen Lord Several hours later, two of the disciples were walking from Jerusalem to Emmaus, about seven miles away, and discussing the events of the previous few days (vv.13-14). Suddenly, Jesus was alongside them —though in some mysterious way they were prevented from recognising him (vv.15-16). When he asked them what they had been discussing, they were amazed that he had not heard the news (vv.17-18). Asked to explain, they told him the whole sad story (vv.19-24). They were sick with sorrow. Still unrecognised, Jesus told them the real cause of their trouble—they had been "sluggish in mind" and "dull of perception" in their understanding of the prophets (vv.25-26 AMP)—or they would have realised that the Christ *had* to suffer before entering into the fulness of his glory (v.26). He then gave what must have been the greatest Old Testament exposition in history—to a congregation of two! (v.27). No wonder their hearts burned within them! (v.32) By now, they were approaching Emmaus, and Jesus accepted their invitation to stay with them (vv.28-30). They sat down to a meal together and suddenly, as he broke the bread and gave thanks, they recognised him — and just as suddenly he disappeared (v.31). But they had *seen him!* – and from then on, nothing would ever be the same again. Knowing facts about Jesus is not enough to save a man, as he himself once made perfectly clear (see John 5.39-40). True Christianity demands a living encounter with its Founder — see 2 Timothy 1.12 — and such an experience is gloriously possible because he is alive today.

"Jesus our Lord . . . was delivered over to death for our sins and was raised to life for our justification" (Romans 4.24-25 NIV).

62
The End Of The Beginning
Luke 24.33-53

Luke's narrative comes to an end in a perfect climax, which we can summarise in four separate paragraphs.

The Agreement Of The Stories We begin at Emmaus, with two disciples staring at an empty chair in which Jesus had been sitting a moment earlier! Although night was falling (see v.29), they immediately turned back to Jerusalem (v.33)—seven miles along a country road lit only by the moon. They found a number of disciples gathered together (v.33) but before the two travellers could get a word in, the others burst out "It is true! The Lord has risen and has appeared to Simon" (v.34 NIV, and see 1 Corinthians 15.5). The two from Emmaus then told their story—down to the last detail! (v.35). Their breathless evidence has since become the testimony of countless millions who have had a life-changing encounter with the living Christ.

The Appearance Of The Saviour As they were talking together, Jesus suddenly appeared (v.36). They were terrified at first, thinking that they were seeing a ghost (v.37) — perhaps because Jesus had mysteriously got into the room through locked doors—see John 20.19. It is marvellous to notice that Jesus's first concern was to reassure them, and replace their fear with faith (vv.38-40). A ghost has neither flesh nor bones; and we are clearly told in the Bible that life after death includes the resurrection of the *body* (see Job 19.25-26 and 1 Corinthians 15.35-38). Their reaction to this challenge is described perfectly — "they still could not believe it for sheer joy" (v.41 AMP). Their emotions swamped their reason! Jesus then asked for some food, and ate it in their presence (vv.41-43)—not to meet his needs, but to meet theirs! Peter was to remember this detail vividly